THORBURN'S BIRDS AND MAMMALS

Stoat, Weasel, Badger and Mole

Hare Studies

THORBURN'S BIRDS AND MAMMALS

John Southern

DAVID & CHARLES
Newton Abbot London

To my mother and father, who first introduced me to Archibald Thorburn amid the pages of a boyhood bird book almost fifty years ago.

And to my wife Barbara, and sons Malcolm, Graham and James, without whose unerring encouragement and support during the past twenty-five years the Thorburn Collection would not have been formed nor Thorburn's work made available to the public.

British Library Cataloguing in Publication Data

Southern, John
Thorburn's birds and animals.
1. Thorburn, Archibald 2. Animals in art
I. Title II. Thorburn, Archibald
759.2 ND1942.T/

ISBN 0-7153-8830-4

Typeset by Typesetters (Birmingham) Ltd, Smethwick, West Midlands
and printed in The Netherlands
by Royal Smeets Offset BV, Weert
for David & Charles Publishers plc
Brunel House Newton Abbot Devon

Contents

Acknowledgements 6
Foreword by David Shepherd, OBE 7
Author's Preface 9
Introduction 11
List of RSPB Christmas Cards 24
A Century of Prints and Proofs 26
Pictures exhibited at the Royal Academy 27
Books illustrated by Thorburn 28
Chronology 32

THE PAINTINGS

Iceland Falcon (1885) 32
Greenland Falcon (1885) 32
The Fallen Beech (1886) 34
The King of Birds (1899) 36
Surprise 36
Sunrise over Gaick (1904) 38
Gleaning after the Shooters (1906) 40
Disputed Rights (1901) 40
Lost in the Glen (1897) 42
Redstarts (1917) 44
The Covey at Daybreak (1892) 44
Blackcock Fighting (1901) 46
The Home of the Golden Eagle (1927) 48
The Shadow of Death (1893) 48
The Lost Stag (1899) 50
Eagle Owl (1917) 52
Morning (1901) 52
Mountain Hare and Irish Hare (1919) 54
Dormice (1903) 56
Clearing after Rain (1905) 56
On the Stooks (1902) 58
Sparrow-hawk (1923) 60
Killed as He Reaches Cover (1906) 60
The Twelfth (1906) 62
Greenland Falcon (1913) 64
A Hard Winter (1907) 64
Watched from Afar (1910) 66
Wrens at the Nest (1923) 68
Over the Hedge (1907) 68
Winter's Sunset (1910) 70
Great Tits (1917) 72
Peacock and Peacock (1917) 72
The Bridle Path (1910) 74
The Finches (1915) 76
Winter Tracks (1913) 76
The Morning Call (1911) 78
The Forester's Friend (1925) 80
Eiders and Scoters (1921) 80
Danger Aloft (1927) 82
Blue, Marsh and Long-tailed Tits (1924) 84
A Frosty Dawn (1927) 84
Through the Snowy Coverts (1926) 86
The Common Squirrel (1903) 88
The Upland Stubbles (1920) 88
Woodcock and Chicks (1932) 90
Ptarmigan at Sunrise (1910) 92
Voices of the Forest (1912) 94
Woodcock Glade (1923) 96

Studies of Thrushes

Acknowledgements

Few books are the work of one person. This one certainly is not. Without the generous help of very many people it simply could not have been compiled.

Space does not permit me to mention personally every individual who has, in one way or another, contributed either towards the formation of the Collection over the years or with the compilation of this book. However, whilst I name but a few, I do thank very sincerely many others.

To those who wish to remain anonymous but who have generously loaned their pictures, either to the museum or for inclusion in this book, enabling others less fortunate than themselves to view and enjoy them, I offer a very special thanks. To Gary Batten I am much indebted for his meticulous help in researching and listing the books Thorburn was involved in, either as illustrator, author or both. Brian Booth of the Tryon and Moorland Gallery similarly assisted in helping to compile as accurate and up-to-date catalogue of prints produced from Thorburn's work, both during his lifetime and since, as is possible, even though new examples from the past continue to appear from time to time. To him also I am most grateful. And members of the Thorburn family have for long been staunch supporters of our efforts on Thorburn's behalf, as have Richard Green and William Marler.

I hope then that the combination of all these interests, efforts and contributions will enable the book to bring the work of this remarkable man, largely owned by the relatively fortunate few, into the homes of the many.

Foreword

I have an unbounded admiration for those relatively few really great wildlife artists of the past who achieved real distinction. Perhaps the greatest African wildlife artist of all time, Wilhelm Kuhnert, did not have the advantage of a Land-Rover, or a camera with a high-powered telefoto lens. Similarly, Archibald Thorburn, a contemporary of Kuhnert's, did not have the advantages that we have in this modern age.

Not only do I admire Thorburn as one of the greatest bird artists of all time, but I have a special interest because as I paint in my studio in Hascombe, I can actually look through the window and see his house where he achieved so many of his great works. As the cars and heavy freight vehicles thunder past my studio down the narrow road (no wider than it was in Thorburn's day), I reflect on those days at the turn of the century when the local residents could well have seen this splendid gentleman with a beard and cloak riding around the lanes of Surrey in his pony and trap. He loathed motor vehicles.

As a painter myself of wildlife subjects, I know that there is no better way of working than from life. For me, sadly, it is not easy to take a canvas and oil paints and set it up in front of an elephant, especially if it is about to charge! Working in the heat of the moment on location gives one that extra physical involvement with the subject. Whether it is Constable, Thorburn, and, dare I suggest it in such company, myself, I know this is true. To my mind Constable's best sketches were those done in the middle of a cornfield when it was about to pour with rain and he had to work fast. Thorburn would go up by train on the long slog, in those days, to Scotland and be met by his friends with a pony and trap. Then, daily, he would drive out along the shores of Loch Maree, surely one of the loveliest parts of Scotland, and one of my own favourite painting haunts, and spend hours out on the moors. This would be hard enough with oil paints. With watercolours, it would be infinitely harder – the elements can damage a watercolour so terribly easily. He would work with his faithful spyglass searching for the details of not only the birds that he loved and knew so well, but the landscape. He never used a camera. He knew, as I do now, how important it is to get the landscape around the animal or bird correct. He was not just an illustrator of birds. He was a wildlife and landscape painter. Just as much dedication would surely be spent on sketching with watercolours and pencil a particular piece of rock, heather, gnarled piece of wood, or a tree in the wide open landscape of his beloved Scotland as the nuances of light and shade on the glistening feather of a pheasant, or the sleek fur of a rabbit in the snow – all would be recorded, the hard way. Then all these treasures gleaned from experience, and perhaps a little suffering in the elements, would be incorporated into his studio masterpieces, so many of which appear in this magnificent book. They breathe the very fresh air of Scotland at its most beautiful.

The Kuhnerts and Thorburns of those days were made of sterling stuff. Now, as a modern-day artist, I almost feel ashamed at just how soft and cushy perhaps life has become. However, I feel sure that I can speak for all present-day wildlife artists when I say that, surely, we can only feel admiration and a great debt of gratitude for what Thorburn and his all too few contemporaries gave us. Their works are now treasures from which we can learn so much.

DAVID SHEPHERD, OBE
1986

Grouse

Partridge

Author's Preface

I first discovered Archibald Thorburn when, as a small boy of eight, I flicked through the pages of T. A. Coward's *Birds of the British Isles*, given to me by my parents as a Christmas present. Good at art at school (though little else!) and interested in wildlife from my earliest days, wildlife art had even then begun to absorb me intensely.

Stumbling across Thorburn that day, I still recall my sense of awe and wonder at the sheer clarity and 'realness' of his rendering of a goldfinch upon a thistle head. More than forty years later, that early enthusiasm and admiration for his abilities has, far from waning, simply grown relentlessly, causing me to devote much of my life and even more of my money towards forming the Thorburn Museum and Gallery, where, gathered together under one roof, some 200 of his finest achievements are now permanently on view for all who wish to see them.

After more than forty years of rummaging through cupboards, attics and cellars, of scrutinising almost every sale in the land, of visiting numerous other private collections and of collecting every book he illustrated, I have to admit complete amazement at the steady yet continuing flow of previously unknown works that appear in the auction rooms year by year, as if Thorburn were still tucked away somewhere hard at work. The man's output was simply prodigious and yet retained the consistent quality that so distinguished his work.

His work always was popular and consequently much in demand, even in his lifetime, but appearances of his pictures in the salerooms today cause an even greater excitement as an ever increasing number of people jostle to own a work by the master.

For me, as for many others, Thorburn's work continues to stand crisply apart from other wildlife artists for a variety of reasons. Accepting his undeniable skills as draughtsman, colourist and naturalist, his paintings overflow with other less obvious ingredients that nevertheless between them bring forth the unmatched flavour and realism of his work. The sense of the unknown, nature's narrative that so often has to be carefully unwrapped, his enviable success with space leading our eye cleverly into the distance and his realistic renderings of time and weather. His pictures vividly recall for us sounds and smells of the countryside too. One is aware of the quiet of the vast isolation of Gaick broken only by an eagle's cry or the scent of the blackthorn in which the bullfinch hides. One never sees him struggling; in fact just the reverse as we become aware of his remarkable understanding of colour harmony and of his skilful reliance upon the progression of one colour, dexterously coaxing it to give up all its tones upon one page as he camouflages the creatures of the countryside amongst their habitat.

The magic of that goldfinch upon the thistle head now so long ago remains crystal clear and quite untarnished in my memory. Far from being simply a painting, it was a revelation of how art and science could blend to produce the truth. Even after a hundred years or more Thorburn's pictures remain brimful of a strange, undying freshness and vitality uncaptured by others that the passing years have done nothing to dim. Nor does it seem are they likely to – at least not for me.

JOHN SOUTHERN

1986

If there should be a sound of song
Among the leaves when I am dead,
God grant I still may hear it sped.

JOHN DRINKWATER

Introduction

Archibald Thorburn, 1860–1935

For he painted the things that matter,
The tints that we all pass by,
Like the little blue wreaths of incense
That the wild thyme breathes to the sky;
Or the first white bud of the hawthorn,
And the light in a blackbird's eye;

ALFRED NOYES

'Thorburn was the greatest ornithological artist superior to all contemporaries in the same field, with a wonderful gift for placing his bird subjects in harmonious surroundings. Whether he was painting a large picture of a whole covey or flock of birds or merely a scientific depiction of a single bird for a book illustration, his method and execution were equally admirable. His birds were never flat maps of plumage, but were essentially solid, with the correct amount of light and shade and reflected lights and colours, always extremely well drawn. He was an excellent landscape painter, and painted flowers just as well as birds. His sketches of plant life, foliage, spray of blossom and such like were extremely clever and beautiful. He appeared to visualise a subject so well before beginning to paint it that his work was very rapid, and wonderfully fluent and direct. His technique was dexterous and bold and his colour brilliant and always harmonious whilst his treatment of the plumage of birds themselves was most remarkable. Thorburn was a man of most lovable qualities, very modest about his work, but never reticent about his own methods of producing it, and always ready to impart his knowledge to others in a most generous way.' So wrote George Lodge, himself a bird artist of great distinction, following the death in 1935 of his lifelong friend and contemporary, Archibald Thorburn. Although some fifty years have now passed since that declaration, Thorburn's reputation as the greatest wildlife painter Britain has ever produced remains unchallenged, indeed unchallengeable.

Unlike most artists, Thorburn received outstanding recognition and acclaim during his lifetime and by the tender age of thirty, in 1890, was already acknowledged as without equal in his field. Since his death this reputation has not only remained secure, but has been much strengthened by the passing years, spreading throughout Europe and across the world. His fame has also expanded from the narrower confines of wildlife art to encompass the whole arena of watercolour painting, where his skills and techniques are now looked upon as equal, if not superior, to many of the already accepted masters of this medium.

Archibald Thorburn was born on 31 May 1860 at Lasswade, a hillside hamlet, near Edinburgh. He was the fifth son of Robert Thorburn, himself an artist of considerable accomplishment, who had graduated from drawing in coloured chalks on the pavements of his home town of Dumfries as a small boy to becoming one of the leading miniaturist painters of his day, much favoured by royalty. He painted a number of portraits of various members of the Royal Family, including Queen Victoria herself, and Her Majesty's favourite picture of Prince Albert – a charming study which she resolutely kept upon her sidetable and which can be seen in several of the Jubilee photographs of the royal couple. Robert Thorburn was born in 1818, moving to London in 1836. Here he was honoured by being made an Associate of the Royal Academy some twelve years later and was held in high esteem as a miniaturist painter of great distinction. In 1858,

Thorburn at about the age of sixty

Thorburn and his wife Constance in their garden at Hascombe with their dog Jock

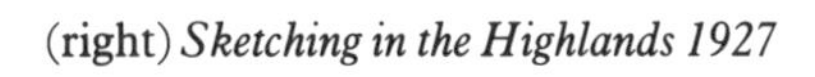

(right) *Sketching in the Highlands 1927*

(left) *Thorburn and one of his brothers in Thorburn's garden at Hascombe*

(right) *The Last Years*

(below) *Thorburn (second left) and his brothers with their mother*

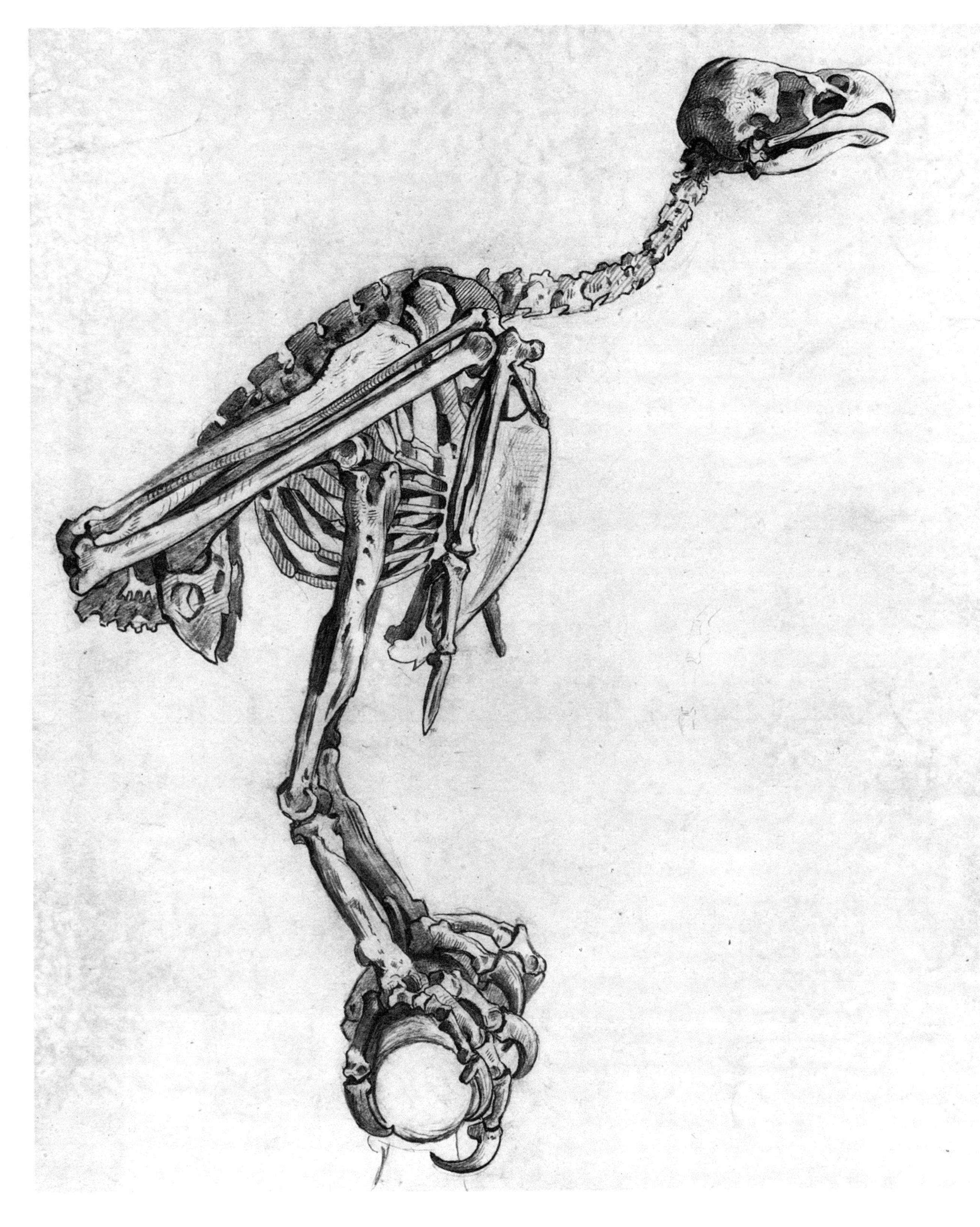

however, he and his wife returned to Scotland, to Lasswade in fact, where, in 1860, Archibald was born. Their home there, Viewfield House, was a spacious and elegant middle-class property which, judging from its name, enjoyed extensive views over the surrounding Scottish countryside. Sadly, all that remains today as a tentative reminder of those times and the family home is a road sign 'Viewfield' – amid just one more estate of modern bungalows. Robert Thorburn died in 1885, but not before imparting much of his skill as an anatomical draughtsman and painter of fine detail to his pupil son. Archibald, at that time in London at art school in St John's Wood, missed his father greatly and was often to acknowledge throughout the rest of his life, his gratitude for his father's teaching, strict and remorseless as it was, particularly his insistence on the basics of anatomy, form and composition.

Much to his father's pleasure, the young Archibald had shown an artistic ability from a very early age, regularly drawing twigs and leaves and flowers from the garden at Viewfield House. Indeed much of his very earliest output had been of flowers and not birds, and this early love never left him for rare indeed is the picture, be it of bird or beast, book illustration or large commission, that is not decked out with some floral embellishment. These environmental hints, a spray of blackthorn or a withering thistle – all add to the charm and accuracy of his work. But Thorburn often told of how his father would almost methodically appear dissatisfied with his son's attempts, regularly tearing up work with which the youngster had been well pleased. Perfection was called for, nothing less and whilst somewhat distressing and certainly frustrating at the time, Thorburn persevered with great patience and self-control, all the while endeavouring to do better and thus please his scholarly father.

Following his father's death Thorburn lived in London, first at 88 Fellows Road just around the corner from the Primrose Hill studio of Joseph Wolf, an artist much admired by both Thorburn and Lodge who rated him the finest draughtsman of wildlife the world had ever seen. Thorburn took lessons from Wolf, a kindly old man, and his influence upon both young artists can be clearly seen in their work of this period. Joseph Wolf died in 1899 and his advice and instruction were sorely missed by them both.

It was in 1889, at the age of twenty-nine, that Thorburn was to arrive at Gaick in Inverness-shire for the first time. He was a guest at the shooting-lodge on the estate and, along with other members of the party, was to stay for several weeks. He at once fell in love with the wild remoteness of the place, the sheer desolation and majesty of towering hills and gaping glens moved him visibly, so much so that they were to feature prominently in his work throughout the rest of his life. He was to return time and time again to this beautiful, desolate place, replenishing his sketchbooks and recharging his enthusiasm to paint ever finer and greater pictures of such scenery, and the birds and beasts of its wilderness. It was here on this first visit in 1889 that he encountered and drew his first wild red deer. Many of his subsequent paintings of deer were composed from sketches made at Gaick and on the surrounding hills and slopes (see 'The Lost Stag', 'Lost in the Glen' and 'Disputed Rights' on pp51, 43 and 41 respectively).

Thorburn was a religious man, and his routine was to labour for six days and rest upon the Sabbath. At Gaick, for six days he had toiled to the tops with the sportsmen, intent upon seeing and drawing his first live ptarmigan at close quarters. Each day the birds were disturbed in advance of the shooting party, leaving but a glimpse of them drifting away across a scree or disappearing over the ridge of a corrie. Disappointed, his hosts told him that the best day to see them would be undoubtedly Sunday, when the shooting party recuperated and relaxed at the lodge. With the Sabbath much on his mind, he rose early and, slipping out at first light, set off up the hill. After no more than half a mile or so he encountered several ptarmigan at close quarters. He returned delighted, with sketches under his arm, and quickly slipped back between the sheets before his colleagues awoke. Most of his ptarmigan, many red deer and not a few golden eagle pictures were drawn at Gaick – most carry a pointed hill in the distance, a sure sign they originated at this place he loved so much (see 'Sunrise over Gaick', 'Ptarmigan at Sunrise' and 'Voices of the Forest' on pp39, 93 and 95 respectively).

Coming down from Gaick back towards Kingussie and habitation, the cart-track snakes its lingering way through the glen, accompanied all the way by the cascading tumbling torrent of the river, finally emerging into Glen Tromie. Here Thorburn often saw and drew blackgame, abundant in his day, and spent many hours sketching them sparring at the lek or packing before the setting sun in winter. Blackgame held a particular fascination for Thorburn all his life and he readily admitted that, along with woodcock, they were his favourite species. He revelled in the challenge of capturing in watercolour their blue-sheened plumage, particularly against the snows of winter as they winged homewards through the woods at dusk. He was also enthralled by the huge packs of a hundred birds or more as they plundered the harvest fields of long ago, perched atop and amongst the stooks of oats (see p59). Thorburn loved Scotland immensely and although resigned, but content, to spend most of his life close to London, he returned to the land of his birth as often as he could.

Before the turn of the century, whilst still a comparatively young man, he was often the guest of a lawyer who lived at Inveran on the shores of Loch Maree in Ross-shire. Here at the home of Mr John Henry Dixon, he was to spend some memorable painting sojourns, enjoying the company of both man and beast at this wild and remote spot. Thorburn would take the train to Achnasheen, to be met there by Hector McKenzie, valet to Mr Dixon. Then by pony and trap they would journey by Loch Maree, past Tolley Woods (right) and on to Inveran. Mr Dixon's dogs, Dot and Doll, feature often in his pictures of that time, and it was here that much of Thorburn's work depicting grouse drives with beaters and the dogs (Dot and Doll) was drawn. His larder paintings too of dead game – blackgame and grouse, hare and deer, were invariably dated before 1902 and were drawn whilst staying at Inveran. In his early years, often whilst staying there, Thorburn regularly composed his pictures of flying birds, in particular, large in the landscape resembling bombers swooping low over the surrounding countryside (see illustrations on p18). In 1902 Inveran was sold and Thorburn was never to return to this wild and beautiful spot that he loved so much. Mr Dixon moved south to Pitlochry in Perthshire and purchased Dundarach. Thorburn continued to stay with him right up until his death in 1926, often calling and staying a week or so with Mr Dixon on his way home from Gaick,

or perhaps from one of his other favourite spots – on the Helmsdale maybe where blackgame abounded, or the Findhorn, where many of his breathtaking wildfowl on the shore studies were first drawn. With Mr Dixon's death and Inveran and Dundarach gone as painting venues, Thorburn still maintained his love affair with Gaick until, in 1930, at the age of seventy and far from well, he found

such journeys too exhausting and thereafter rarely left his Hascombe home.

In 1896 Thorburn married Constance Mudie, daughter of Charles Edward Mudie of the lending library fame, and in the same year appointed A. C. Baird-Carter, who had just opened a gallery at 61 Jermyn Street, SW1, as his picture agent in London. Shortly after the turn of the century Baird-Carter moved to larger premises on the opposite side of the street and it was at 70 Jermyn Street that Thorburn was to sell his pictures throughout the rest of his life.

In general he enjoyed a good working relationship with Baird-Carter in spite of some early disagreements and as his pictures were already in such demand, he was able to drive a hard bargain with his agent. Although shy and retiring by nature, his shrewd Scottish business sense proved more than a match for any dealer seeking a quick fortune from an unsuspecting, yet up and coming, young artist. It was Baird-Carter who conceived the idea of an annual Christmas card that was to prove so popular over the years. These were octavo in size and the first one, published in 1899, was of a cock pheasant in the branch of a tree. The Greenland falcon shown on page 64 was the one he painted for Christmas 1913, and it must surely be one of his finest.

In 1919 Baird-Carter died and was succeeded by William Fraser Embleton, already well known to Thorburn, for he had been apprenticed to Baird-Carter and later became his assistant. Embleton and Thorburn were to become good friends as well as successful business associates. Each fortnight Embleton would journey to Hascombe to spend the day with Thorburn. He would take paints and paper ordered by Thorburn and return with finished watercolours, commissions for waiting clients. Embleton was one of the favoured few allowed to sit and watch Thorburn painting. Normally the studio was out of bounds to all but his wife and a handful of his closest friends. Embleton, however, on his fortnightly visits, would sit behind Thorburn's left shoulder and watch the master at work.

Thorburn's method and speed of work was remarkable. He appeared to visualise a scene clearly in his mind before he began and, with the briefest of pencil strokes, quickly marked out the composition, perhaps a pack of ptarmigan amongst the screes of Gaick. Referring to sketchbooks, first of the birds and then of the terrain, he would carefully yet quickly copy the selected sketches on to the picture under composition. Having lightly constructed the picture in this way, on would go the colours. First the broad washes of sky, background, foreground and birds. Almost before it was dry the next layers would be laid down and his standard commissions, measuring very close to 7in × 10in and 10in × 15in, were nearly always completed in a day and even his impressive imperials would rarely take him longer than a week from start to finish. On these occasions, whilst he painted, Thorburn would converse with Embleton and invariably the talk would turn to an elaboration of the waiting list. How many people were waiting for a picture, who they were and what subjects they had specifically requested. Month by month and year by year the list grew longer and whilst impossible to promise firm dates for all those patiently waiting – many being the aristocracy of the time – Thorburn could always be relied upon to produce a picture for a special occasion, such as a wedding, a birthday or anniversary.

Whilst retaining first Baird-Carter and then Embleton as his principal agent throughout his life, Thorburn's shrewd business sense led him to believe, however, that it would be wise for him not to depend entirely upon one agent in London, but to appoint others in more distant areas of prosperity. So it was that R. Haworth of Blackburn and

Mawson, Swan & Morgan in Newcastle were appointed; Thorburn regularly called upon them, delivering a batch of watercolours to each in turn, often on his way north to Scotland or perhaps breaking his journey homewards.

In 1898 Thorburn was elected a Fellow of the Zoological Society and almost thirty years later he became a vice-president of the Royal Society for the Protection of Birds (RSPB), an honour that gave him particular pleasure for, although a sportsman and a good shot in his early days, by 1927 he had been a staunch supporter of conservation and bird preservation for many years. He had painted the society's very first Christmas card in 1899 and went on to produce some eighteen more, ending with one of a goldcrest in 1935 – completed literally weeks before his death on 9 October of that year. Each of the RSPB Christmas cards was accompanied by a verse, the first, in 1899, by the Poet Laureate, Alfred Austin. All the cards are beautiful but the ones he painted during World War I are particularly moving and poignant – the robin perched upon the snowbound cross of 1917, symbolising the Resurrection (see p24); (Thorburn had felt that a Red Admiral butterfly rather than a robin would have been more appropriate) and the 1918 skylark, rising from amid the dead of battle, to tower and pour out its song high above the debris of war.

In spite of his work being selected to hang in the Summer Exhibition at the Royal Academy in 1880 when he was a mere twenty years old and still very much an unknown artist, to be followed by another nineteen, Thorburn was never to be elected even an Associate of the Royal Academy let alone receive full Royal Academy status. The Summer Exhibition of 1900 was to witness his last huge and compelling entry for the Royal Academy for, after twenty years of exhibiting there, he was considerably disillusioned and disappointed at the way his pictures had invariably been hung – so high and difficult to see, making it impossible for them to be properly assessed and appreciated. Furthermore the demand for his work was, by 1900, increasing at such a rate that he largely had to forgo these huge and majestic watercolours in order to keep anything like abreast of the order book. His entries for the academy, usually of grouse, eagle, blackcock or partridge, and always enormous by watercolour standards, were remarkable achievements. Carefully drawn, skilfully composed and painted with great flair, confidence and originality, they were technically brilliant accomplishments. Indeed, for sheer technical brilliance he was probably never to outpaint them ('The Lost Stag' p51). These paintings, together with other very large pictures painted before or around the turn of the century and at the time of his first visits to Gaick and Inveran, have a quiet and distinctive charm and quality all of their own ('The Shadow of Death' p49). They are never forced or contrived, nor laboured, nor repetitive, but spectacular and spontaneous results of an inspired young painter, who had for the first time filled his lungs with the fresh air billowing across the wildest and remotest places in Britain and was keen to record all he saw in the way he knew best.

When he returned to his studio in London, or Hascombe, he then converted his lovely pencil drawings made on the hill or in the glen into these really quite marvellous finished watercolours. How fortunate we are, a hundred years on, that Thorburn's inspiration enabled him to paint with such conviction, composure and control, pictures of Britain's wildlife we have not seen the like of since.

In 1902 Thorburn and his wife moved from London to Hascombe in Surrey, purchasing a substantial residence (recently completed) nestling in this lovely unspoilt village. Here at High Leybourne, he was to spend the rest of his life, working quietly yet diligently amid the rolling countryside he grew to love so much. Far from the madding crowd and the rumble and roar of the

outside world, and yet within easy reach of his dealer's shop in Jermyn Street, it proved an idyllic setting for such a shy and retiring painter, and especially for a man who shunned publicity. High Leybourne extended in all to some fifteen acres and Thorburn had a gate-house built in the grounds for his widowed mother enabling her to live nearby. She, also, moved to High Leybourne in 1902, and lived there peacefully, visited each day by her devoted son, until her death in 1908. She was buried in the churchyard of nearby Busbridge, and Thorburn chose to be interred within the same grave some twenty-seven years later.

His studio, out of bounds to all but the favoured few, was spacious with a large window looking out upon his garden. He invariably painted at an easel, seated upon a cushion atop an old black stool, his Winsor & Newton paintbox flanked by three water bowls to his right and, to his left, different sizes of paper were kept neatly stacked upon shelves. Sometimes whilst engaged upon a work, he would take a small piece of paper from one of the shelves and place it towards the edge of his drawing board and try out a position of a grouse maybe; it would perhaps be changed two or three times before finally deciding if and how to construct it within the particular picture. Many completed pictures, mounted though not yet framed, were stacked against the walls – Thorburn mounted all his own work but left his agent to undertake the framing.

In a small room adjoining the studio was a sink with a cold water tap only used to draw water for painting and to wash out his brushes, and an ingenious escape door which, by all accounts, was much used. The scheme worked as follows. Thorburn would be busily at work in his studio wishing for no interruptions. However, quite often the door bell would ring. Moments later Mrs Thorburn ushered the uninvited guest along the hallway towards the studio and exclaimed, in a louder voice than usual, 'How nice to see you again Mr . . . !' Thorburn meanwhile, poised from his painting since the ring of the bell, would listen intently. If the voice was that of a dear friend then all was well. But, if the guest was not only uninvited but also unwelcome Thorburn would quickly and silently let himself out into the garden, through the escape door, and sit there shielded by some shrubs and quietly wait for the danger to pass. On the inside of this useful door always hung a roll of cartridge paper from which Thorburn would cut his standard sizes upon which to paint, together with a selection of nails and leather straps, amongst which some of his tools of the trade would be neatly kept.

Thorburn was very much a man of routine, rising at 7.30am each day and breakfasting at 8.30am. Breakfast always included porridge made from the best Scottish oats which he had specially sent down from his homeland. The papers would arrive with the milk and he would read these before taking a walk around his extensive and very beautiful garden, of which he was passionately fond. He returned to the studio, and the day's work began at 9.30am, and he would then paint continuously until at least 12.30pm, when luncheon was always served. Usually several calls, five or so minutes apart, each one more shrill, were needed to persuade him to wash out his brushes and heed the call, even though baked apple and cream – his particular favourite – was invariably upon the menu. Following lunch, afternoons would again be spent energetically painting and, in the quiet of the evening, another stroll around the garden, but this time with his wife. The day would usually end promptly at 10.30pm when the oil lamps were extinguished and they retired to bed. Every so often this routine would be broken by a walk through the woods of Juniper Valley just beyond his garden gate, or at Dunsfold perhaps, where, armed with pencil and sketchbook he gathered material from life for future finished pictures, capturing the postures and patterns of pheasant and woodcock, squirrel and fox with lightning ease. On his way home he would sometimes call at the village shop to purchase an item or two, and once there could be gently persuaded to turn the pages of his delightful sketchbook disclosing all the creatures he had seen upon his walk. Thorburn had a great dislike of the motor car and totally distrusted electricity, having nothing to do with either throughout his life. Transport to and from the nearby town of Godalming, as well as through the surrounding countryside, was by pony and trap. The gardener also took Thorburn's only child, Philip, to Charterhouse School by this means. Lighting at High Leybourne was to remain by means of oil lamps throughout his life, though Mrs Thorburn was quick to modernise the system shortly after his death. Thorburn is remembered with much affection by some now elderly people who recall the gentle white-haired gentleman who would call at the village school at Hascombe and with lightning speed and amazing agility, draw birds and animals with chalk upon the blackboard.

Although shy, Thorburn was always ready to impart his knowledge and endeavour to share his skills with those who sought it, just as others had helped him when he was young. Several young bird artists of the time took tuition from the master, notably Philip Rickman, whose work bore much of Thorburn's influence upon it. Many of Britain's bird artists, since Thorburn, owe much to him, either directly as a result of lessons he gave them or indirectly from simply admiring and being influenced by his work. Indeed can any wildlife artist

since Thorburn truthfully say he or she has not been influenced in one way or another by the skills, subtleties and techniques of Thorburn? Philip Rickman who died in 1982, aged ninety-one, admired him enormously, marvelling at his draughtsmanship and skills as a colourist. He often told of Thorburn's incredible speed of execution, deftly hinting at this and that without actually painting it. Rickman recalled Thorburn repeatedly emphasising that the most important part of the bird to paint correctly is the part you cannot see! Referring as he was to the three-dimensional aspects of the bird, involving a considerable skill in foreshortening in order to 'form' it correctly, quite often, Thorburn watched dutifully over Rickman's shoulder, aware of the young man's difficulty as he struggled to achieve this 'shape'; then he would quickly and politely ask Rickman to move aside, whereby Thorburn himself would immediately sit down at the work, and with, quite literally, no more than two or three brushfuls of paint bring forth life to the creature, giving it body and making it solid simply through the use of light and shade. He excelled at painting the eyes and feet of birds, areas that trouble many artists and his birds and mammals are always beautifully balanced. Standing well, their centres of gravity perfectly in place. He was exceptionally clever at generalising, being able to achieve a brilliant effect of larch trees or bracken, or spray of blackthorn by the merest touch and cleverest hint. Whilst saving hours of detail work the result of this approach and technique is of a strange freshness and vitality even after all these years, uncluttered and unburdened with heavy detail.

As an illustrator Thorburn had no equal. One only has to contemplate the timelessness, the beauty and accuracy of his book plates to see why this is so. Illustrations he painted a hundred years ago are still being reproduced today in bird identification books, they are the most widely reproduced bird paintings of all time. The eighty-two glorious plates he painted for his own four-volume book, *British Birds of 1915–16*, with their unerring accuracy and charm, softness of form and sparkling with vitality, have also enjoyed an amazing revival and success in recent years, the book being reprinted in popular form by Michael Joseph and proving to be an immediate best seller. These particular plates are

also fine examples of his mastery of composition, encompassing as they do a veritable galaxy of species upon almost every page. Yet each picture remains uncluttered and each bird retains its independence, often accompanied by a delightful hint of its environment to set it apart from the others (see 'The Finches' on p76).

His very first coloured illustrations appeared in 1883 (one of which is illustrated above), when he was but twenty-three years of age, and his last, posthumously, in 1937 and 1938, several years after his death. During the intervening years he illustrated innumerable titles (see p28), and his artistic talent and services were greatly in demand as principal illustrator for many of the fine natural history books of the late Victorian and Edwardian eras. From his charming grisaille works for the *Fur, Feather and Fin* series, *Autumns in Argyllshire* and other books from around the turn of the century (see illustrations overleaf), through to his carefully painted colour identification plates and on to his free flowing, pulsating environmental masterpieces in his *Gamebirds and Wildfowl of Great Britain and Northern Ireland* of 1923, each was unmistakably by his hand – each was a breath of fresh air in what was otherwise a largely unimaginative and negative period for bird art. Thorburn's great friend and contemporary George Lodge was perhaps the principal exception to this rule, for he too was portraying birds as they had never been seen before.

Thorburn's earliest achievements did not pass unnoticed by Lord Lilford of Northampton who at that time had recently embarked upon a major new work to be entitled *Coloured Figures of the Birds of the British Islands.* J. G. Keulemans, the popular bird artist of the day, had been commissioned to paint the pictures for this monumental work but, unfortunately, he fell ill and was unable to continue the task. Keulemans' misfortune became Thorburn's opportunity of a lifetime for he went on to paint some 268 scintillating watercolours for the book – taking him in all ten years to complete. The first plates by Thorburn – the mallard and some of the other ducks – for Lord Lilford appeared in September 1888. The book was issued in parts between 1885–1898. Never before had such beautiful pictures of Britain's birds been seen. Superbly balanced, correctly feathered and delicate to the touch, they were technically perfect and a joy to behold, being so far removed from anything that had been seen before. The book had not been selling too well until the appearance of the Thorburn plates when the demand for it dramatically increased threefold. Thorburn had, in those first few carefully painted pictures, immediately established himself not only as the foremost bird artist of the day but also as someone very special indeed, the like of whom may well be seen only once during many lifetimes (see the 'Greenland Falcon' and 'Iceland Falcon' on p33). This huge and demanding commission over, Thorburn settled down to a variety of illustrative work for several leading authors of the day, as well as a veritable stockpile of commissions from private clients that had steadily amassed during his years of toil for Lilford.

It was not until 1915 that the first of Thorburn's own books appeared, both illustrated and written by him. The paintings for *British Birds*, issued in four volumes, together with a supplement, were

begun in 1912 and are still regarded by many as the most beautiful plates of British birds ever painted. Although a book on the identification of birds, almost all of the eighty-two plates are adorned by the discreet inclusion of some botanical specimen, be it in a wood, upon a moorland or even on the shore. The success of *British Birds* brought forth other books written and illustrated by Thorburn in quick succession, all published by Longman Son & Green, of Paternoster Row, with whom he enjoyed a long standing and successful relationship. In 1919 *A Naturalist's Sketch Book* was published, followed a year later by *British Mammals* containing the most truly accurate and delightful pictures ever painted of the mammals of our countryside (see the 'Mountain Hare and Irish Hare' on p55). The bats deserve special mention as do the dolphins and whales, which although he found difficult are immensely successful. In the introduction to his *Gamebirds and Wildfowl of Great Britain and Northern Ireland* of 1923 Thorburn wrote 'My aim in this work has been to represent these birds grouped in their natural surroundings rather than to make scientific plates of the species'. This he most certainly achieved, excelling himself with incredibly free and natural pictures. In 1925 a completely rewritten *British Birds* was published containing 192 lovely watercolours specially painted for the book. Now octavo in size and in four volumes, the new plates were less crowded than those of the 1915–16 book, with often only one or two species on each page, unlike the quarto edition of ten years earlier. Some of Thorburn's last published illustrations appeared in 1937, two years after his death and signified a remarkable achievement. Not only were they painted by an old man, frail and far from well, and from skins of birds he had never seen alive in the field or even at the zoo, but the backgrounds were constructed from vestiges of botanical specimens forwarded to his studio at Hascombe from the Sudan, accompanied by brief notes regarding the terrain and the temperature of the place. The authors of the book – Archer & Godman, never ceased to marvel at the remarkable, indeed uncanny, accuracy of the plates that resulted; the arid heat of the desert, the dust, the nature of the vegetation and the posture of the birds, all exactly lifelike.

During the years of preparation and painting for his own books there is a noticeable shortage of other significant works. For instance, important pictures of gamebirds or stags dated 1913–16 are virtually non-existent, for at that time he was very busy on the eighty-two plates for his 1915–16 *British Birds*, as well as writing the text. At the peak of his career Thorburn was producing between a hundred and a hundred and fifty finished pictures each year. Towards the end of his life, however, Embleton confirmed that this had dropped to perhaps sixty or so, causing even further congestion on the waiting list.

With the exception of Thorburn, few bird artists have had the ability to portray all types of birds with equal ease. Whilst undoubtedly best known for his paintings of gamebirds, where without question he remains in a class of his own, Thorburn was nevertheless able to move from blackgame to blackbird and swiftly on to buzzard with the utmost ease, conviction and success. His song birds were outstandingly beautiful and successful, an area that troubles more than a few artists but Thorburn was able to capture their delicacy and charm and their lightness of weight with few strokes but great truth. His wildfowl were equally as pleasing and his best birds of prey were without equal, his Greenland falcons being as awe-inspiring as the living creatures themselves. The bird he found most difficult to paint was the robin, although few would criticise his lovely rendering of such a familiar bird in the RSPB Christmas card of 1917. Thorburn equally excelled

at his painting of mammals, his mice and hedgehogs, hares and foxes in winter and of course his wild red deer are all a delight to behold. His love of and ability to paint flowers is obvious and, although rare in his paintings, he incorporated a charm into the painting of butterflies, successfully capturing their delicacy and frailty. Thorburn's fluency across the wide spectrum of nature was indeed remarkable, all aspects however mundane and trivial, being dealt with in the same accomplished, positive yet unburdened way.

Thorburn's sketchbooks, of which he filled many during his lifetime, are a sheer delight. A few light strokes of his pencil not only amply reflected his technique and enquiry but also captured the whole personality of the creature as well. Many show his painstaking determination to get the drawing right, several attempts were perhaps made at the wing of the great tit whilst hanging upside down, or the head of the red grouse whilst feeding. Each though was spontaneous, an echo from nature that Thorburn received clearly and was able to transcribe on to paper equally as clearly. Thorburn freely admitted that he quite often found it difficult to capture again that spontaneity, as the drawing was carefully transferred from sketchbook to commissioned picture upon the drawing board. Sadly, some of his sketchbooks were destroyed by his wife shortly after his death, as she believed they would be of little value. Fortunately, during a bonfire in the garden, many were literally rescued from the fire by a friend who happened to call at that very moment.

During the time before Thorburn, with the exception of Wolf, bird art had been at best adequate but more often ugly and unacceptable. Awkward in stance and tiled in feathers, the birds had so obviously been painstakingly plucked from long since stuffed specimens, complete with no sense of gravity, badly faded soft parts and no true hint of their environment. Thorburn, even as a very young man, was fully aware of this situation as he was equally ill-at-ease with much of the work of his predecessors; he found it awkward and unlifelike. It was this that persuaded him to attempt a totally different approach whereby he believed every single item, from pebble to ptarmigan, should be drawn out in the field and from life. Since Thorburn we have seen a multitude of bird artists, some more

obviously under the influence of Thorburn than others, gaining a more secure and long lasting reputation, but most giving their birds so many feathers that they would have the utmost difficulty in achieving lift off! So many make the mistake of burdening the birds, and the landscape, with detail to the extent that they appear to be endeavouring to improve upon nature and, as a consequence, their work is totally unreal. Thorburn's twigs, branches, and leaves were rarely found neatly yet tiresomely linked together, but rather painted as impressions of foliage, with many bits and pieces left suspended in mid air (see 'Woodcock and Chicks' on p91). His creatures were convincingly framed by light and shade rather than cluttered with detail. It is his 'impressions' of the countryside that make his work so real and fresh.

In the hundred years that have elapsed since the world first gasped at Thorburn's skills, what is it about his work that ensured his unrivalled reputation in this field? Perhaps if we clinically dissect one of his pictures and then piece it together again we may find the secret. Unlike many, Thorburn begins a picture from the baseline of reality. All the elements to be incorporated within the painting would have been seen and drawn first-hand in the wild. Not only the creatures and the environment of the painting, but also the angle of the land and the intensity of the light would have been recorded. This framework of having been there and seen the creatures, having heard the grouse and smelt the heather, not forgetting the lie of the land and the play of light upon all it touched, these things immediately thrust Thorburn well ahead of the rest in the initial stages of constructing a painting. After referring to sketchbooks (as seen on the left), he was then able to place his subjects realistically, being fully aware of how they group or fly, feed or doze. Satisfied with the drawing, his scientific knowledge coupled with his remarkable artistic skills, particularly at generalising, ensured accurate pulsating creatures unburdened with detail. Swift and fluent and bold with colour the picture would quickly take shape. Finally, one of Thorburn's great gifts was knowing when to stop; when to wash his brushes out and declare the picture finished. So many artists add more and more until the picture topples over from success to mediocrity or even failure.

Thorburn has left us with painted memories of the best-loved scenes from our past. His output is brimful of fresh and vibrant recollections of nature in all her varied moods. Whilst his winter pictures bring a chill to all who stand before them, absorbing the bleakness of the situation and noticing the footprints in the snow, one revels in the warmth and renewal from his glorious pictures of autumn, among the heather on the hill or amid the burnished larches along the woodland ride. His long inquisitive years devoted to unravelling nature's secrets enabled him beyond all others to capture in paint not only the posture of the birds and animals but even their personalities. Nothing was too big or too small to attract his attention and deserve his sympathy. With his faultless technique coupled with the field knowledge of an expert, his pictures are the perfect example of art and science working hand in hand. Such well-blended masterpieces had certainly not been seen before Thorburn and few, if any, have been seen since. Thorburn's pictures recall for us a tranquil, leisurely, gentle age when the countryside slumbered, still unaware of the devastation that was soon to befall it as the century unfolded. Hedges would be hacked out – taking with them the nesting places of partridge for one – as the call for greater farming efficiency went out. Now we are so efficient we have mountains of food that nobody wants – apart from the starving whose cries seem to go unheard – and the partridge and the dormouse and a myriad of other creatures dependent upon the trusty English hedgerows for their survival have all but gone. Partridge abounded in Thorburn's day, almost tumbling over themselves. Now they have almost vanished from our countryside. His pictures are a timeless reminder of the way things were when the countryside at least was at peace.

As the years continue to pass by, Thorburn will long be remembered not only for his sheer artistic mastery and skills that have forever set him apart from others, but for such telltale touches as the few shed feathers – the withering thistle – the footprints in the snow – all hallmarks of his observation and an affinity with the countryside, unknown but to a few.

Thorburn contracted cancer in 1929, and in 1930 endured a major operation to remove the growth. He was to survive for a further five years, bearing his burden of pain and discomfort with characteristic cheerfulness and quiet determination as the wound upon his back refused to heal. Each day was painful, some excruciatingly so, but he never complained. During this period he continued to paint as before and produced many pictures, nearly all of which retained their remarkable consistency of quality, and each flowed with clarity and freshness. His pictures still appealed to all who saw them, for they so vividly retold of the creatures one was likely to encounter on a typical countryside walk. Some pictures of this period of course show signs of advancing years and increasing pain, the draughtsmanship was perhaps a little less certain and the paint applied with just a hint of unease in the hand. The heads of the grouse were a little woollier than before and the background less distinct. Yet this late work was still stamped with his greatness that makes it so distinctive.

He continued to produce pictures for prints with Embleton almost to the very end of his life, the final one echoing his very first, portraying his beloved blackgame. The last one, showing blackgame in winter, somehow seems to foretell of the bleak times ahead both for the artist and all those who had grown accustomed to his revelations of the countryside in paint and who were going to have to become accustomed to there being no more. The last picture he was to paint was of a goldcrest, painted whilst lying in bed. It was also to be his last contribution to the RSPB – their 1935 Christmas card – the nineteenth he painted for the society since his first almost forty years earlier. The picture took several days and needed much effort and determination on the part of the dying man. But each day he would call for his paints and, propped up in bed, concentrate for an hour or so until he felt too tired to continue. During the last few weeks he was confined totally to bed and a series of private nurses lived at the house and tended him. Each confirmed the stories of the others, as they told of his gentlemanly qualities, his courteousness and cheerfulness. As one puts it '. . . he was so well endowed with old world courtesy and still had a delightful twinkle in his eye. A truly wonderful gentle gentleman.' Every morning, however unwell he felt, he would call for his white hair to be neatly combed and brushed and his equally white beard to be trimmed. As the nurse who was with him at the end recalls 'Mr Thorburn kept himself immaculate right up to the day of his death'. He was most grateful to these ladies for the loving care and attention they had bestowed upon him and to show his appreciation, invited them to go down to his studio and select any picture as a keepsake before they left. Each then returned to his room to gain approval of their selection before bidding him farewell.

At his committal, in Busbridge churchyard on 13 October 1935, the Reverend Newton Jones read a prayer he had specially composed for the occasion thanking God 'for the gifts with which Thou did'st endow our departed friend; for the seeing eye and the steady hand; for his gifts of vision and imagination; for his insight into the beautiful world which Thou hast made; the pictures which brought joy and inspiration into so many lives. We thank Thee not only for the beauty which he created with brush and pen. We bless Thee still more for the beauty of his life. We remember before Thee with deep gratitude his utter goodness and spirituality, his simplicity, humility and goodness, his generous and affectionate nature . . .'

List of RSPB Christmas Cards painted by Thorburn and donated by him to the Society

1899	Roseate Terns. (Accompanied by a verse by the Poet Laureate)
1905	Blackbird
1916	Whitethroat
1917	Robin. *Behind the Lines*
1918	Skylark. *No-man's Land*
1919	Ringed Plover. *First Impressions*
1923	Goldfinch. *King Harry*
1924	Bullfinch (on blackthorn). *John Bull*
1925	Greater Spotted Woodpecker. *The Forester's Friend*
1926	Redstart. *The Fire-tail*
1927	Grey Wagtail
1928	Nuthatch. *Britain's Blue-bird*
1929	Sandpiper by water
1930	Wheatear. *The Herald of Spring*
1931	Oystercatchers. *Sea-Piets*
1932	Stonechat on bracken stem
1933	Chaffinch. *The Bachelor's Finch* (Original presented to King George V)
1934	Longtailed Tits
1935	Goldcrest

1899

1905

1916

1917

1923

1924

1926

1928

1931

1935

A Century of Prints and Proofs of Thorburn's Work (1885–1986)

1885–6 'Summer Days' – partridge and young, Lawrence & Jellicoe (colour)
1885–6 'Leaving Covert' – cock pheasant, Lawrence & Jellicoe (colour)
1885–6 'Rising from the Reeds' – mallard drake, Lawrence & Jellicoe (colour)
No date 'Capercailzie', Lawrence & Bullen (sepiatone)
No date 'Woodcock', Lawrence & Bullen (sepiatone)
No date 'Snipe', Lawrence & Bullen (sepiatone)
No date 'Blackgame', Lawrence & Bullen (sepiatone)
No date 'Partridge', Lawrence & Bullen (sepiatone)
No date 'The First Far Away Echo' – fox, Lawrence & Bullen (sepiatone)
1889 'Grouse Driving' – the end of the line, E. E. Leggatt (etching)
1892 'Ptarmigan on Snow Slip', Unknown (sepiatone)
1892 'Out of the Valley of Death', Leggatt Bros (sepiatone)
1893 'Partridge Shooting' – breaking up the covey, Leggatt Bros (sepiatone)
1894 'Grouse by the Peat Pool', Fine Art Society (colour)
1894 'Partridges in Snow' – with bullfinch, Fine Art Society (colour)
1894 'Grouse Drive', Leggatt Bros (sepiatone)
1895 'Out in the Cold' Fine Art Society (sepiatone)
1895 'First Sight of the Beaters', Fine Art Society (sepiatone)
1895 'Courting', Fine Art Society (sepiatone)
1895 'The Last of the Flush', Fine Art Society (sepiatone)
1895 'Uninvited Guests', Fine Art Society (sepiatone)
1895 'Good Beat Spoilt by Fox', Fine Art Society (sepiatone)
1896 'The Home Coverts', Leggatt Bros (sepiatone)
1896 'Grouse', *Illustrated London News & Sketch* (colour)
1896 'The First Victim', *Illustrated London News & Sketch* (colour)
1896 'Driven Partridges', *Illustrated London News & Sketch* (colour)
1896 'Pheasants Feeding', *Illustrated London News & Sketch* (colour)
1896 'Driven Grouse', *Illustrated London News & Sketch* (colour)
1896 'Waiting for the Turn of the Tide', *Illustrated London News & Sketch* (colour)
1896 'Woodcock and Chicks', *Illustrated London News & Sketch* (colour)
1896 'The Frozen Spring' – snipe, *Illustrated Sporting & Dramatic News* (black & white)
1896 'Grouse at the Drinking Pool', *Illustrated Sporting & Dramatic News* (black & white)
1896 'The First Woodcock', *Illustrated Sporting & Dramatic News* (black & white)
1896 'On the Wall' – blackgame, Fine Art Society (black & white)
1896 'Home Life' – red grouse, Fine Art Society (black & white)
1896 'Blackcock Forward', Fine Art Society (black & white)
1896 'A Hare Drive', Fine Art Society (black & white)
1896 'Partridge and Young by Brambles', Fine Art Society (black & white)
1896 'Partridge and Two Hares driven before Beaters', Fine Art Society (black & white)
1896 'Pheasants', Fine Art Society (black & white)
1899 'Stags, Hinds and Golden Eagle', Thomas Bain (black & white)
1899 'Going Down Wind' – partridges, Leggatt Bros (black & white)
1899 'Coming over the Guns' – partridges, Leggatt Bros (black & white)
1900 'Among the Stubble' – partridges, Leggatt Bros (black & white)
1900 'Grouse Shooting – Put up by the Beaters', Mawson, Swan & Morgan (black & white)
1900 'Partridge Shooting' – 'The Last Bit of Cover', Mawson, Swan & Morgan (black & white)
1900 'The Twelfth', Lawrence & Bullen (black & white)
1900 Partridges in stubble, Leggatt Bros (colour)
1901 'An Improvised Drive' – blackgame, Fine Art Society (sepiatone)
1901 'Some Shootable Beasts' – stags, Fine Art Society (sepiatone)
1901 Partridges and goldfinch, Baird-Carter (colour)
1902 Grouse calling, Baird-Carter (colour)
1903 'A Haven of Rest' – woodcock, Baird-Carter (sepiatone)
1903 'The Open Spring' – snipe, Baird-Carter (sepiatone)
1903 'The Glory of Autumn' – pheasants, Lawrence & Bullen (black & white)
1903 Woodcock & robin, Baird-Carter (colour)
1903 Capercailzie in Scots pine, Baird-Carter (colour)
1903 Grey and French partridge, Baird-Carter (colour)
1903 Wigeon and teal, Baird-Carter (colour)
1903 Ptarmigan on the tops, Baird-Carter (colour)
1903 Blackcock in flight, Baird-Carter (colour)
1903 Woodpigeons in beech tree, Baird-Carter (colour)
1903 'The Twelfth' – grouse over the moor, Baird-Carter (colour)
1903 Pheasants in the snow, Baird-Carter (colour)
1903 'The First Arrival' woodcock and oyster-catcher, Baird-Carter (colour)
1903 Mallard in winter, Baird-Carter (colour)
1903 Golden plover, Baird-Carter (colour)
1904 Jack snipe, Baird-Carter (black & white)
1904 'The Swamp where humm'd the Dropping Snipe', Baird-Carter (black & white)
1904 'Hungry Woodcock', Baird-Carter (black & white)
1904 'A Labour of Love', Baird-Carter (black & white)
1904 Pheasants in winter, Baird-Carter (colour)
1905 'Straight for the Butts', Baird-Carter (black & white)
1905 Mallard in flight, Baird-Carter (black & white)
1905 Lapwing and golden plover, Baird-Carter (colour)
1906 Teal, Baird-Carter (black & white)
1906 Pintail and wigeon, Baird-Carter (black & white)
1906 Pintail, wigeon and teal, Baird-Carter (colour)
1907 Golden eagle, Baird-Carter (colour)
1907 'Frost in the Coverts' – pheasants, Baird-Carter (colour)
1907 'The Close of a Winter's Day' – partridge, Baird-Carter (colour)
1907 Set of six red deer of Scotland, Baird-Carter (colour)
i 'Shadowed'
ii 'The Peat Hag'
iii 'Disputed Rights'
iv 'Changing Quarters'
v 'After the Mist has Lifted'
vi 'The First Snow on the Tops'
1908 Peregrine falcon on teal, Baird-Carter (colour)
1909 'The First of September', Baird-Carter (sepiatone)
1909 'The Sentinel' – red grouse, unknown (colour)
1909 Ptarmigan in the snow, Baird-Carter (colour)
1910 Snipe in the reeds, Baird-Carter (colour)
1911 'Amongst the Heather', Baird-Carter (sepiatone)
1911 Blackcock at the lek, Baird-Carter (colour)
1912 'Fox Grove', Baird-Carter (sepiatone)
1912 Partridges dusting, Baird-Carter (sepiatone)
1912 Mallard on the lake at Sandringham, Baird-Carter (colour)
1913 Greenland falcon, Baird-Carter (colour)
1914 Woodpigeons on beechmast, Baird-Carter (colour)
1915 Cock and hen bullfinch, Baird-Carter (colour)
1916 Goldfinches on thistles, Baird-Carter (colour)
1917 Wigeon and teal, Baird-Carter (colour)
1918 'The Windfall' – Fox and dead pheasant, Baird-Carter (colour)
1919 Goldeneye and tufted duck, Baird-Carter (colour)
1919 Set of twelve birds of prey, limited 150 sets, Baird-Carter/Embleton (colour)
i 'Marsh Harrier'
ii 'Golden Eagle'
iii 'Sparrowhawk'
iv 'Honey Buzzard'
v 'Peregrine Falcon'
vi 'Merlin'
vii 'Montagu's Harrier'
viii 'Goshawk'
ix 'Red Kite'
x 'Iceland Gyr Falcon'
xi 'Hobby'
xii 'Kestrel'
1920 Oystercatcher, terns and ringed plover, Baird-Carter/Embleton (colour)
1921 'Frozen-out Fisherman' – kingfisher, Embleton (colour)
1921 'Grouse over the Burn', Embleton (colour)
1921 Winter blackbird, Embleton (colour)
1921 Pheasants, Embleton (colour)
1921 Jay, Embleton (colour)
1922 Wigeon over the estuary, Embleton (colour)
1922 Pintail on the shore, Embleton (colour)
1922 Mallard on the shore, Embleton (colour)
1922 Blue tits on the teasel, Embleton (colour)
1923 Snipe probing, Embleton (colour)

1923 Woodcock, Embleton (colour)
1923 Cock and hen redstarts, Embleton (colour)
1923 Golden eagles at the eyrie, Embleton (colour)
1924 Robin and wren, Embleton (colour)
1925 Blackcock through the silver birches, Embleton (colour)
1925 Pheasants through the oak wood, Embleton (colour)
1925 'September Morning' – partridges, Embleton (colour)
1926 Shoveler by the mere, Embleton (colour)
1927 Grouse over the moor, Embleton (colour)
1927 Partridges and young, Embleton (colour)
1927 Mallard in squally weather, Embleton (colour)
1927 Wigeon alighting, Embleton (colour)
1927 Grouse sheltering, Embleton (colour)
1928 Partridges in the stubble, Embleton (colour)
1928 Nuthatches, Embleton (colour)
1928 Summer kingfisher, Embleton (colour)
1928 'Sunshine and Drift' – ptarmigan, Embleton (colour)
1929 House martins, Embleton (colour)
1930 Great tits and mistletoe, Embleton (colour)
1931 'The Old and the New' – pheasants, Embleton (colour)
1932 Grouse in the peat bogs, Embleton (colour)
1933 Woodcock and dog violets, Embleton (colour)
1934 Blackgame in winter, Embleton (colour)
1974 Red squirrel, Edition of 250, Tryon Gallery Ltd (colour)
1975 Longtailed tits, Edition of 500, Tryon Gallery Ltd (colour)
1975 Winter woodcock, Edition of 500, Tryon Gallery Ltd (colour)
1975 Amid the Highlands, Set of six prints Edition of 500, Tryon Gallery Ltd (colour)
 i 'Voices of the Forest' – red deer
 ii 'Overlooked' – roe deer
 iii 'Danger Aloft' – ptarmigan
 iv 'At the Break of Day' – red grouse
 v 'The Glen among the Moors' – blackgame
 vi 'The Eagle's Eyrie' – golden eagle
1978 'The First Touch of Winter' – pheasants, Edition of 500, Tryon Gallery Ltd (colour)
1978 'September Siesta' – partridge, Edition of 500, Tryon Gallery Ltd (colour)
1982 'The Drove Road' – red grouse, Edition of 500, Tryon Gallery Ltd (colour)
1982 'Autumn Woodcock', Edition of 500, Tryon Gallery Ltd (colour)
1982 Wren, Edition of 500, Tryon Gallery Ltd (colour)
1982 Blue tits, Edition of 500, Tryon Gallery Ltd (colour)
1983 Game birds – set of four prints, Edition of 500, The William Marler Gallery (colour)
 i 'Watched from afar' – pheasants
 ii 'The Home of the Red Grouse' – red grouse
 iii 'Sunrise over Gaick' – ptarmigan
 iv 'At the edge of the Stubble' – partridges
1986 British game birds – set of eight prints, Edition of 400, Malcolm Innes Gallery (colour)

Pictures exhibited at the Royal Academy by Thorburn

Date	Exhibition Number	Title
		THORBURN, Archibald . . . Painter.
1880	714	'On the Moor'
	824	'The Victim'
1881	751	'A Christmas Hamper'
1882	959	'Blackgame'
	972	'The Twelfth of August'
	981	'The First of October'
1883	999	'The Golden Eagle'
1885	1328	'Undisturbed'
1887	1213	'The Eagle's Crag'
1888	1249	'The Covey at Daybreak'
	1324	'Blackgame Disturbed'
1890	1327	'The Pack at Sunrise'
1892	921	'The Last Drive'
	1203	'Eagles disturbed in their Nest'
1893	549	'A Grouse Drive'
	977	'Golden Eagles on the Watch'
1894	1079	'The Lost Hind'
1895	920	'The Watchful Hinds'
1898	1054	'The Home of the Golden Eagle'
1899	1128	'The Lost Stag'
1900	1195	'The Eagle's Stronghold'

Books illustrated by Thorburn's Plates, Drawings & Woodcuts

The following is an alphabetical-by-author list of books illustrated by Thorburn, and of some later books in which his work has been reproduced. (Also included are some books and articles containing text only, considered collectable by Thorburn *afficionados* because they contain material of special significance regarding Thorburn.)

Anker, Jean. *Bird Books and Bird Art: An outline of the history and iconography of descriptive ornithology* (Levin and Munksgaard, Copenhagen, 1938, 251pp. With a facsimile reprint pub. Junk, The Hague, 1973.)

Archer, Sir Geoffrey Francis and **Godman**, Eva Mary. *The Birds of British Somaliland and the Gulf of Aden* (Gurney and Jackson, London, 1937 (vols 1 and 2); Oliver and Boyd, London, 1961 (vols 3 and 4), 626pp. Contains Thorburn's last published plates. Drawings based on two of the plates in this work were used on four postage stamps of the Somaliland protectorate issued in September 1953; these being Somali rock pigeon (Somali stock dove) on the 35 cents and 2/- values and Martial eagle on the 50 cents and 5/- values [see also **Jackson**, C. E.].)

Attenborough, David. *Thorburn's Mammals* (Ebury Press and Michael Joseph, London, 1974, 128pp, being a reduced format version of *British Mammals*, 1920–21 (see **Thorburn**) containing all fifty plates of the original with notes by Iain Bishop. Further edition 1979 with a new edition in paperback 1983, Mermaid Books, and a further hardback edition in 1984, Peerage Books.)

Barnes, J. A. G. [see **Coward**, T. A.]

Beebe, C. W. *A Monograph of the Pheasants* (Witherby, London, 1918–22; 4 vols, 913pp, nintey colour plates, some of the finest of which are by Thorburn (others by Lodge, Grövold et al.).)

Beebe, C. W. *Pheasants, their lives and homes* (1926, 2 vols, containing some colour and some monochrome reproductions of plates from the above work.)

Benson, S. Vere. *The Observer's Book of British Birds* (Warne, London, 1937 (with many subsequent reprints and editions). The most popular book containing many Thorburn plates from 'Lilford' (1885–98) 224pp. [In later editions some of Thorburn's *Corvidae* plates are replaced by those of Robert Gillmor and Ernest C. Mansell.])

Blagdon, F. W. *Shooting, with game and gunroom notes.* 1900 (decorative boards).

Blyton, Enid [see **Coward**, T. A.]

Brander, Michael (editor). *The International Encyclopedia of Shooting* (Pelham, London, 1972. Contains enlarged and coloured reproduction of an original Thorburn monochrome plate depicting blackcock which was first used as a frontispiece to '*Autumns in Argyllshire . . .*' [see **Gathorne-Hardy**]. A later edition, published by Peerage Books, contains the same plate, and also one colour plate from *British Mammals* (1921) and two plates from *British Birds* (1915–18).)

Buxton, Sydney Charles (Earl Buxton). *Fishing and Shooting* (John Murray, London, 1902, 269pp. Contains three Thorburn monochrome plates depicting aspects of fishing and three on shooting.)

Cardew, Jeremy. *Thorburn's Wildlife* (Windward, Leicester, 1979, 160pp. Contains Thorburn illustrations from *A Naturalist's Sketchbook* (1919), *British Birds* (1915–18) and *British Mammals* (1920–21) both coloured and black & white, with a text by Jeremy Cardew, FRES, ARCS.)

Clifford, Derek. *Collecting English Watercolours* (John Baker, London, 1970, 143pp. One monochrome reproduction of a study of the plant 'Old Man's beard' by Thorburn, signed and dated 2 Jan 1924.)

Coward, Thomas A. *The Birds of the British Isles and their Eggs* (Warne, London, 1920–6, 1070pp, in three volumes. This book, which uses many of the Thorburn plates from 'Lilford' (1885–98), has enjoyed many editions, each of which has run into several reprints. Some significant editions are cited here . . . 1950 (seventh) edition with a revised text by A. W. Boyd, 3 vols. 1969, a new edition in one volume with revised text by J. A. G. Barnes in which some of Thorburn's plates are replaced by those of Gillmor, Mansell etc. Running concurrently with these from 1937 onwards was a pocket-sized version, edited by Enid Blyton and titled *Birds of the Wayside and Woodland*. In this edition rarer species were omitted.)

Coward, Thomas A. *Bird Haunts and Nature Memories* (Warne, London, 1922, 214pp. Thorburn monochrome frontispiece of noctule bat, dated 10 October 1919.)

Coward, Thomas A. *Bird Life at Home and Abroad, with other Nature observations.* (Warne, London & New York, 1927, 242pp. Coloured frontis by Thorburn as *Flamingoes at Home*.)

Dale, Thomas Francis. *The Fox* (Longmans, Green & Co, London, 1906.[*Fur, Feather & Fin* series No 12] 238pp. Contains vignette and six monochrome plates by Thorburn. (The two remaining plates being by G. D. Giles.) This series had a standard (5/-) edition in buff cloth, pictorial boards, and a de-luxe (7s 6d) edition, green, half-bound and top edges gilt. There are twelve volumes in the series and Thorburn had illustrations in all but the three volumes dealing with fish [see also **MacPherson, Shaw** and **Harting**].)

Dance, S. P. *The Art of Natural History* (1978, 224pp. Contains colour and monochrome plates by Thorburn.)

Dewar, George Albemarle Bertie. *Life and Sport in Hampshire* (Longmans, Green & Co, London, 1908, 274pp. Two colour plates by Thorburn, being: frontis, 'Orange-tip butterfly and Speedwell' and, to face page 190, 'Six-spot Burnet moths and Knapweed'.)

Dougall, Robert. *Thorburn's Naturalist's Sketchbook* (Michael Joseph, London, 1977, 136pp. Reduced format of the 1919 edition [see **Thorburn**] with additional plates from *British Mammals* (1920–21) and *British Birds* (1915–18).)

Dresser, Henry Eeles, **Sharpe**, Richard Bowdler, and **Hay**, Arthur, Viscount Walden. *A History of the Birds of Europe, including all the species inhabiting the Western Palæarctic Region* (Published by the authors. London, nine volumes (including the Supplement), originally published in 93 parts (5,144pp) between 1871–81 [96]. Supplement of 1895–6 contains colour plates by Thorburn.)

Drewitt, C. M. *Lord Lilford, . . . Thomas Littleton, Fourth Baron, . . . A Memoir by his Sister [Hon Mrs F. Dawtrey Drewitt]* (Smith Elder, London, 1900, 290pp. Includes seven plates in monochrome, by Thorburn, of Lilford Hall, Northamptonshire and living birds in its aviaries.)

Eden, R. *Going to the Moors* (John Murray, 1979. Coloured frontis by Thorburn.)

Fisher, James. *The Birds of Britain* (Collins, London, 1942 (Britain in Pictures Series No 36) 48pp. Contains one colour plate (red grouse) and one monochrome plate (red-breasted mergansers) from Millais' . . . *Game Birds* (1909) and . . . *Diving Ducks* (1913) respectively.)

Fisher, James. *Thorburn's Birds* (Michael Joseph, London, 1967, 184pp. Contains all eighty-two plates from *British Birds* (1915–18) [see **Thorburn**] with updated text, reduced format and plates rearranged into more modern order. Reprints 1971, 72, 74. Revised edition 1976 with reprints 1977 and 79. A new edition in paperback 1982 (Mermaid Books) and a further edition in hardback by Peerage Books, London, 1985.)

Fisher, James. 'Archibald Thorburn' (*Birds* (RSPB) mag. 12(1) 258–62. Four colour plates taken from *Thorburn's Birds* [see above] Nov– Dec issue 1967.)

Fraser Darling, Frank. *Wild Life of Britain* (Collins, London, 1943 (BIP No 52) 48pp. Contains one Thorburn colour plate, one monochrome plate and two pen drawings. These being from Millais' . . . *Mammals* and Thorburn's . . . *Mammals*.)

Fulcher, Florence Anna. *Birds of Our Islands* (Andrew Melrose, London, n/d (but 1897) 368pp. Two bindings known: Light-blue, and buff, decorative boards. All edges gilt. Contains numerous woodcuts from 'Swaysland' and three monochrome plates depicting little terns, sub-adult golden eagle and peregrine. The latter two are wrongly captioned as 'Whitetailed Eagle' and 'Merlin'. Thorburn's name has been erased from these plates.)

Gathorne-Hardy, Hon Alfred Erskine. *Autumns in*

Argyllshire with Rod and Gun (Longmans, Green & Co London, 1900, 228pp. Monochrome frontis depicting black grouse [see entry under **Brander**] and seven other mono plates depicting: wild cat, roe deer, red deer, cormorants and seals, salmon fishing, pointers working and snipe shooting.)

Gladstone, Hugh S. *Handbook to Lord Lilford's Coloured Figures of the Birds of the British Islands* (Bickers, London, 1917, 69pp. (Text only.) (An essential book for those wishing to understand the chronology of the various parts of this great work.))

Gladstone, Hugh S. 'Obituary. Archibald Thorburn', *Scottish Naturalist* 1936 ((217) pp1–7. A lengthy, though interesting item of text.)

Gordon, Lord Granville. *Sporting Reminiscences* (Grant Richards, London and E. P. Dutton, New York, 1902, 209pp. Contains two sepia plates by Thorburn depicting the Morsgail stag and red grouse.)

Graham, P. Anderson. *Country Pastimes For Boys* (Longmans, Green & Co London, 1897, with new editions in the same year and in 1908, 448pp. Decorative boards, all edges gilt. Contains two plates by Thorburn of partridge and red grouse from the *Fur, Feather & Fin* volumes dealing with those species.)

Grahame, Major Iain. *Thorburn's Birds of Prey* (A facsimile of the rarest Thorburn book [see entry under **Thorburn**]. Published by Major Grahame on 9 October 1985 to commemorate the 50th anniversary of Thorburn's death. 32pp. Like the original, this work was limited to 150 copies, fifteen of which are full bound, and the remainder half bound. The book contains the twelve plates, twelve pages of text and H. S. Gladstone's introduction of the original plus a new foreword by Major Grahame.)

Grimble, Augustus. *Shooting and Salmon Fishing – some hints and recollections* (Chapman & Hall, London, 1892.)

Grimble, Augustus. *Highland Sport* (Chapman & Hall, London, 1894.)

Grimble, Augustus. *The Deer Forests of Scotland* (Kegan Paul, Trench, Trübner & Co, London, 1896, 324pp. Contains eight Thorburn monochromes.)

Grimble, Augustus. *Deer-Stalking and the Deer Forests of Scotland* (Kegan Paul etc, London, 1901, 343pp. Eight monochromes by Thorburn. [Based on two earlier titles – *Deer-Stalking* (1888) and *The Deer Forests of Scotland* (1896)].)

Grimble, Augustus. *The Salmon Rivers of Scotland* (Kegan Paul etc, London, 1902, 400pp. Illustrated by Thorburn.)

Grimble, Augustus. *Shooting and Salmon Fishing and Highland Sport* (Kegan Paul etc, London, 1902, 275pp. Sixteen monochrome illustrations by Thorburn. [Based on two earlier titles – 1892 and 1894.])
*Large paper editions of the Grimble titles published by Kegan Paul etc, usually numbered 500 copies.

Hamilton, N. *Three Centuries of British Bird Books* (Country Life, 30 Oct 1980. Four colour plates by Thorburn.)

Hardy – [see entry under **Gathorne-Hardy**].

Harting, James Edmund. *Sketches of Bird Life from Twenty years' observation of their Haunts and Habits* (W. H. Allen & Co, London, 1883 (with a further (8vo) edition appearing in the same year) 292pp. The illustrators of this volume are listed thus: 'Wolf, Chas Whymper, Keulemans and Thorburn', though illustrations by other artists also appear. This book contains two monochromes by Thorburn, the first of his plates to be published, though the work of the young Thorburn is greatly over-shadowed by that of some of the other illustrators. The first plate shows a very 'eagle-like' kestrel which appears to be 'falling-over-backwards' from its perch, and the second plate shows a family of blue tits. In this plate, the tail of the main subject appears to originate from its left flank! Thorburn was twenty-three when he drew these plates.)

Harting, James Edmund. *The Rabbit* (Longmans, Green & Co, London, 1898. (*Fur, Feather & Fin* series No 6) 256pp. Monochrome frontis by Thorburn.)

Horsfield, H. Knight. *Sidelights on Birds. An Introduction to the study of British Bird Life* (Heath Cranton Ltd, London, 1923, 224pp. Contains mono plate of peregrine (to face p135) forming the frontis to chapter XIII – being 'The Artist and the Bird'. This plate is one of a series of drawings made of various birds of prey in the gardens of the Zoological Society of Scotland (Edinburgh) on 19 February 1918 (or, more correctly, a series covering mid-February to early March of that year). More drawings from that series appearing in *A Naturalist's Sketchbook* [see **Thorburn**].)

Hudson, William Henry, and **Beddard**, Frank E. *British Birds* (Longmans, Green & Co, London, 1895, 363pp (with subsequent impressions). The eight colour plates are by Thorburn being: golden eagle, bearded titmouse, goldfinch, bittern, teal, ptarmigan, dotterel and roseate tern. This book also contains 108 monochromes by Thorburn's friend and contemporary G. E. Lodge and three photographs by R. B. Lodge.)

Innes-Shand, Alexander. *Mountain, Stream and Covert, Sketches of Country Life & Sport in England & Scotland.* (Seeley & Co, 1897, 336pp. Decorative boards. Contains two Thorburn mono plates. Frontis – wild swans on Loch Spynie and ptarmigan to face p32. (Frontis dated 1897.))

Irby, Lt Col L. Howard L. *The Ornithology of the Straits of Gibraltar* (R. H. Porter, London, 1875. It was the second edition of 1895 (326pp) which contained fourteen plates, of which Thorburn was artist for eight chromolithographs (the remaining plates were from photographs by Col W. W. C. Verner who also contributed to the text of this edition. The Thorburn plates depict various vultures, eagles and falcons, a blue-winged (Azure-winged) magpie and a European bush-quail.)

Jackson, Christine E. *Bird Illustrators. Some Artists in early Lithography.* (Witherby, London, 1975, 133pp. In the section dealing with Thorburn, one reproduction of a Thorburn lithograph (eagle owl) from 'Lilford' and, scattered throughout the book, five woodcuts from 'Swaysland'. A most useful and informative book which had an edition deluxe of forty-five copies.)

Jackson, Christine E. *Collecting Bird Stamps.* (Witherby, London, 1977, 118pp. On p63, a photograph of a Somaliland Protectorate stamp which carries a Thorburn design of a Somali stock dove (as Somali rock pigeon) [see also **Archer**].)

Jackson, Christine E. *Wood Engravings of Birds.* (Witherby, London, 1978, 144pp. (Companion volume to *Bird Illustrators.*) Has Thorburn woodcuts from 'Swaysland'.)

Jenkins, Alan C. *Wildlife in the City. Animals, birds, reptiles, insects and plants in an urban landscape.* (Webb and Bower Ltd, Exeter, 1982, 160pp. Contains a monochrome reproduction of a plate from Millais' . . . *Mammals* depicting black and Alexandrine rats, and a pen drawing of a Scottish wild cat from Thorburn's . . . *Mammals.*)

Keith, E. C. *A Countryman's Creed* (Country Life, London, and Charles Scribner's Sons, New York, 1938, 205pp. The standard (London) edition has a coloured frontis as partridges in Norfolk (dated 1930) and twelve reproductions of pencil drawings, all by Thorburn. An edition de-luxe was produced – limited to 250 copies – it contained nine coloured plates in addition to the pencil drawings.)

Koenig, Alexander F. *Avifauna Spitzbergensis . . .* (Published by the author, Bonn, 1911, 304pp. Contains thirty-four colour plates, twenty-six photographs and a folding map. The colour frontispiece, dated 1910, and depicting little auks, was painted by Thorburn. Also an edition de-luxe having the frontis reproduced on f.bd, heavily embossed in gold.)

Lakatos, Károly. *A Vadászmesterseg Könyve* (Budapest, 1902.)

Lewis, Frank. *A Dictionary of British Bird Painters* (Published by the author, Leighton-on-sea, 1974, 47pp plus plates. One monochrome plate by Thorburn as: 'The Frosty Marshes' (duck).)

Lilford, Baron [Thomas Littleton Powys]. *Coloured figures of the Birds of the British Islands* (referred to elsewhere in this list as 'Lilford'). R. H. Porter, London, 1885–98, thirty-six parts in seven volumes [two editions]. Part i of the first edition is dated October 1885, and part i of the second edition is dated April 1891. The chronology of the two editions is somewhat complex but the later parts of both editions appeared concurrently. In his 'Handbook' to this work H. S. Gladstone [see entry under **Gladstone**] says (p9) '. . . there is no question that the second edition is the more desirable of the two as being the more accurate, and as containing some plates superior to those in the first edition; in fact, roughly speaking, the coloration of about one-third of the plates in the second edition may be said to have been improved. Moreover, the second edition was limited to 450 copies, as compared with 550 copies of the first edition.')

The volumes contain 974pp. *421 plates of which Thorburn was artist of 264 chromolithographs and drawer of four designs after Joseph Wolf (who had himself declined Lilford's request for him to be chief artist on account of his age). Thorburn was brought in to the work of illustration in January 1887, after J. G. Keulemans had been taken ill, and his first plate was published in part vii, volume 2, in September 1888. Keulemans completed 125 chromo plates. Other (named) artists being: William Foster (1 plate), G. E. Lodge* (6), Edward Neale (5) and Joseph Smit (1).
*Lodge's plate depicting the turtle dove gave cause for some complaints from subscribers as the scale and style was not in keeping with that of the other plates, though it was not withdrawn or suppressed by Lilford. Thorburn was asked to produce an additional plate to be sold separately to subscribers who wished to purchase it. Only 100 copies were printed and sold for 12/- each. Consequently, copies of 'Lilford' with the extra turtle dove plate bound-in are very rare. Some examples of plates printed but later suppressed (and therefore not called for in the completed work) are to be found bound into some copies. About twenty examples of such plates (by various artists) are known.

Lilford, Baron [Thomas Littleton Powys]. *Notes on the Birds of Northamptonshire and Neighbourhood*

(R. H. Porter, London, 1895, 2 vols, 667pp, with a large paper edition of 706pp. Twenty-four monochrome plates of birds and Northamptonshire scenery by Thorburn. Other illustrations by G. E. Lodge.)

Little, Alicia Bewicke [Mrs Archibald]. *Our pet Herons* ((R)SPB leaflet No 35, 1900, 4pp. Contains Thorburn monochrome of a group of little egrets.)

Little, Crawford (editor). *Country Sport* mag (March 1985. Has on its cover, a detail from a Thorburn painting of blackgame 'On the Stooks'.)

Little, Crawford (editor). *Country Sport* mag (March 1986. Has on its cover a detail from a Thorburn painting of merlin and in an article on the art of deer stalking by Malcolm Innes, a monochrome reproduction of a painting of red deer.)

Lodge, George Edward [as G.E.L.] 'Obituary' (Archibald Thorburn. *British Birds* 29 (6) 1935: 172. Lodge was born in the same year as Thorburn (1860) but outlived him by nineteen years. The two were great friends, each having admiration for the other's work. In summing up Lodge says: 'His beautiful work has set a very high standard for those who plod in his footsteps in the same line of life; but – there will never be a second Thorburn.' (Text only.))

Lodge, George Edward [as G.E.L.] Archibald Thorburn (Ibid. (13)6(1): 205–6, 1936 (text only).)

Mackenzie, E. G. *In Grouse Land* (1985. Frontis by Thorburn.)

Mackie, Sir Peter Jeffrey, Bt. *The Keeper's Book* (G. T. Foulis & Co, London. First edition 1904 with many revisions, reprints and re-writes. Tipped-in plates by G. D. Armour, Roland Green, Philip Rickman and Thorburn. It is obvious from the dates on some of the Thorburn plates, that they were not present in the earlier editions, ie partridges – to face page 236 – dated 1909, which first appeared in the second reprint (June 1909) of the first 'Revised and Enlarged' edition. Therefore, for those interested in Thorburn's contribution, the later editions are the more collectable (say 1928–9).)

Macpherson, H. A. et al. *The Partridge* (Longmans, London, 1894, *Fur and Feather* (later *Fur, Feather & Fin*) Series No 1, 276pp, nine monochromes by Thorburn.)

Macpherson, H. A. et. al. *The Grouse* (Ibid, 1894, No 2, 293pp, ten monochromes and one vignette by Thorburn.)

Macpherson, H. A. et al. *The Pheasant* (Ibid, 1894, No 3, 265pp, nine monochromes [ten in 2nd edn. 1896] and one vignette by Thorburn.)

Macpherson, H. A. et al. *The Hare* (Ibid, 1896, No 4, 263pp, three Thorburn monochromes.)

Macpherson, H. A. et al. *The Red Deer* (Ibid, 1896, No 5, 328pp, six monochrome plates by Thorburn.)

Mallalieu, H. L. *The Dictionary of British Watercolour Artists up to 1920.* (Antique Collectors' Club, 1976, 557pp, 2 vols. (Vol 1 – The Text, vol 2 – The Plates). Monochrome reproduction of Thorburn watercolour, dated 1923, showing a pair of house martins.)

Mathew, The Rev Murray A. *The Birds of Pembrokeshire and its Islands* (R. H. Porter, London, 1894, pp lii + 131, containing plates, photographs and maps and also having a large paper edition.)

Matschie, Paul. *Bilder aus dem Tierleben* (Union, Stuttgart, 1900, 476pp. Contains some text figures by Thorburn.)

Meinertzhagen, Col R. *Nicoll's Birds of Egypt* (Hugh Rees, 1930, 2 vols. Containing thirty-eight colour plates of which one (Verreaux's eagle) is by Thorburn.)

Meinertzhagen, Col R. *Birds of Arabia* (Oliver & Boyd Ltd, Edinburgh, 1954, 638pp. Containing nineteen colour plates of which one (ringed plover) is by Thorburn.)

Meinertzhagen, Col R. *Birds of Arabia* (Henry Sotheran Ltd, 1986. Edition de-luxe on large paper. Illustrations printed from the original blocks. Edition limited to 295 copies to sell at £298.)

Millais, John Guille. *The Natural History of the British Surface-Feeding Ducks* (Longmans Green & Co, London, 1902, 168pp. Eight colour plates by Thorburn.)

Millais, John Guille. *The Mammals of Great Britain and Ireland* (Longmans, Green & Co, London, 1904–06, 3 vols, 1,048pp. Contains thirty colour plates by Thorburn produced between 1893 and 1905.)

Millais, John Guille. *The Natural History of the British Game Birds* (Longmans, Green & Co, London, 1909, 142pp. Some of the total of eighteen colour plates are by Thorburn.)

Millais, John Guille. *British Diving Ducks* (Longmans, Green & Co, London, 1913, 2 vols, 305pp. Contains fifteen colour plates by Thorburn.)

Millais, John Guille. *Rhododendrons . . . and the various hybrids* (Longmans, Green & Co, vol 1 1917, vol 2 1924, 532pp. Two of the colour plates are by Thorburn.)

Millais, John Guille. *British Gamebirds and Wildfowl* (*The Gun at Home and Abroad*, London, 1912, 455pp. Illustrations by Thorburn, Lodge et al.)

Millais, John Guille *British Deer and Ground Game* (*The Gun at Home and Abroad*, London, 1912.)

Moorland Gallery Ltd. *Archibald Thorburn, Artist and Illustrator* (1974, 34pp. Containing both colour and mono reproductions of Thorburn's work.)

Morgan, A. *Llyfr Adar (Adar Cymru)* (1907. Text in Welsh. Pocket size (7½in × 5in). Thirty-one colour plates by Thorburn and others.)

Mullens, W. H. and **Swann**, H. Kirke. *A Bibliography of British Ornithology . . .* (MacMillan & Co, London, 1916–17, 691pp (text only). Containing many references to Thorburn's work. A facsimile reprint has recently been published.)

Naturhistorisches Museum, Berne. *Der Vogel in Büch und Bild* (Berne, 1954. Contains two monochrome plates by Thorburn.)

Nissen, Claus. *Die illustrierten Vogelbücher ihre geschichte und bibliographie* (Hiersemann, Stuttgart, 1953, 223pp, 4to. Sixteen plates, representing the work of several 'bird artists', also figures in the text. A facsimile of this classic work was published in 1976 (bound in fine green cloth).)

Owen, J. A. 'The Lilford Vivaria' (*Pall Mall* mag. Sept 1896, 48–61). (Six Thorburn monochrome plates illustrate this article; these showing: ravens, goshawks, various falcons on blocks and bow-perches, a falcon 'on the glove', various duck on the pond, and assorted waders in a specially constructed enclosure.)

Owen, J. A. (editor). *Drift from Long Shore* (Hutchinson & Co, London, 1898, 261pp. Monochrome frontis by Thorburn, showing 'Snipe'.)

Peek, Hedley. *The Poetry of Sport* (Longmans, Green & Co, London, 1885 (Badminton Library), 420pp. Five Thorburn monochrome plates showing: golden eagle about to rob ♀ sparrowhawk of prey (teal), mallard, pheasant 'put-up' by spaniel, snipe, and red grouse.)

Powys, Thomas Littleton. [See **Lilford**].

Pycraft, W. P. *Birds of Great Britain and their Natural History* (Williams and Norgate, London, 1934, 206pp. Has, as its frontispiece, a colour plate of ptarmigan taken from 'Hudson and Beddard'.)

Savory, E. W. (editor). *Sporting Pictures* (n/d but probably 1905. One 'shooting' plate by Thorburn.)

Shaw, L. H. de Visme et al. *Snipe and Woodcock* (Longmans, Green & Co, London, 1903. *Fur, Feather & Fin* series No 10, 298pp. Four monochromes by Thorburn and four by Chas Whymper.)

Shaw, L. H. de Visme et al. *Wildfowl* (Ibid, 1905, No 11, 278pp. Four monochromes by Thorburn and four by Chas Whymper.)

Sitwell, Sacheverell, **Buchanan**, Handasyde and **Fisher**, James. *Fine Bird Books 1700–1900* (Collins, London, and Van Nostrand, New York, 1953, 120pp. Although this beautifully produced book does not contain a pictorial example of Thorburn's work it does refer, on pages 45, 72, 83, 91 and 110, to five of the works in which Thorburn was involved ie *British Birds* (1915–18), 'Dresser', 'Irby', 'Lilford' and 'Swaysland'. [See elsewhere in this list.].)

Skipwith, Peyton. *The Great Bird Illustrators and their Art 1730–1930.* (Hamlyn, London, New York etc, 1979, 176pp. Three colour plates from *Thorburn's British Birds* (1915–18).)

Southern, John. *Thorburn's Landscape. The Major Natural History Paintings* (Elm Tree Books/Hamish Hamilton Ltd, London, 1981, 120pp. Contains fifty-one colour plates and figures in the text, spanning the years 1881–1933 and showing the development in Thorburn's work. The book also contains much biographical detail about Thorburn.)

Southern, John. *Archibald Thorburn.* (*Country Sport* mag. 1(1) 31–33, June 1983. Contains four colour reproductions of Thorburn paintings and a photo of Thorburn; also a detail from a Thorburn painting on cover.)

Southern, John. 'Thorburn – the master of a new tradition'. (*Birds* (RSPB) mag. 9(6) 29–31, summer 1983. Four colour reproductions of Thorburn's work.)

Stewart, Henry Elliott. *The Birds of Our Country* (Digby, Long & Co, London, 1897, 395pp. Illustrated boards, top edges gilt. A pretty little book, with illustrations on virtually every other page! Thorburn's woodcuts from 'Swaysland' are used in this work. Other illustrators are: J. Giacomelli, G. E. Lodge, K. Keyl and R. Kretchmer. (All illustrations in monochrome.))

Suffolk and **Berkshire** (Earl of) [editor] et al. *The Encyclopedia of Sport* (Lawrence & Bullen, London, 1897–8 (in two volumes). A new and enlarged edition with colour plates, photographs and drawings (in four volumes) was published in 1911 by Wm Heinemann. The Thorburn monochromes of the first edn. having been colour-washed for this edition (not always to the best advantage – in a plate showing a drake wigeon, the colourist has done his/her best at decking the bird out in the plumage of a drake mallard, and, not knowing quite what to do with the pale head-flash, has left it white!) The fifteen Thorburn plates deal mainly with British/European animals and birds of the sporting field with the exception of a very nice study of sable antelope at a waterhole.)

Swaysland, Walter. *Familiar Wild Birds* (Cassell & Co, London, 1883–8. Four volumes. Decorative boards. 160 colour plates. Published in parts, this work contains (in the first edition) 105 chromolithographs by Thorburn. Later editions had plates reprinted using the three-colour process. In addition to the colour plates there are some beautiful woodcuts from Thorburn originals which, in charm and composition, are better than some of the plates. Other illustrators in this work (plates and/or woodcuts) are: A. F. Lydon, G. E. Lodge, and E. Turck. This book was Thorburn's first major publishing assignment.)

Tate, Peter. *A Century of Bird Books* (Witherby, London, 1979, 256pp. In the sections dealing with Thorburn and with Coward there are black and white photos of the covers of *British Birds* 1925–26, vol IV (puffins) and of *The Birds of the British Isles* . . . vol II (little bustard) plus references in the text.)

Thorburn, Archibald. 'Sabine's Gull in Cornwall' (*Zoologist*, 475–6, 1896.)

Thorburn, Archibald. *British Birds* (Longmans, Green & Co, London etc, 1915–16 (and 1918), 420pp in 4 vols. Eighty colour plates in first edn. Two further plates (80a and 80b) were published in an 11p supplement. These showed new additions to the British/Irish List. Second and third editions had these plates bound-in. One hundred and five copies of each of the four volumes were on large paper. Reprint [see under **Fisher**].)

Thorburn, Archibald. *A Naturalist's Sketchbook* (Longmans, Green & Co, London, 1919, 72pp, sixty plates, of which twenty-four are in colour. Large paper edn numbering 105 copies. Reprint [see under **Dougal**].)

Thorburn, Archibald. *Birds of Prey* (Baird-Carter/Embleton, London, 1919. Published as a set of prints in portfolio, it was left to subscribers whether or not they had these bound into a book. There were twelve plates, each with an accompanying page of text, and an introduction by Hugh S. Gladstone. Only 150 sets were published, and several of these were bound into book form. Over the years, however, some of these have been 'broken' and the plates sold-off thus making this the rarest Thorburn book. A facsimile was published on 9 October 1985 to commemorate the 50th anniversary of Thorburn's death [see under **Grahame**]. The subjects of the twelve plates are: marsh harrier, golden eagle, sparrow hawk, honey buzzard, peregrine, merlin, Montagu's harrier, goshawk, red kite, Iceland gyrfalcon, hobby and kestrel.)

Thorburn, Archibald. *British Mammals* (Longmans, Green & Co, 1920–21, 2 vols, 108pp, fifty colour plates and pen-drawings in the text. Large paper edn numbering 155 copies. Reprint [see under **Attenborough**]. Details from thirty of the plates in this book were used for a set of cards issued, with album, by Grandee Cigars (Imperial Tobacco) in March 1982.)

Thorburn, Archibald. *Gamebirds and Wildfowl of Great Britain and Ireland* (Longmans, Green & Co, 1923, 80pp. Contains thirty colour plates. Large paper edn numbering 155 copies.)

Thorburn, Archibald. *British Birds* (Longmans, Green & Co, London, 1925–6, 4 vols, 638pp. Bibliographically the fourth edition of Thorburn (1915–18) with an octavo format and 192 new colour plates by the author. Large paper edn had 205 copies.)

Thorburn, Archibald. 'Kittiwakes nesting in Dunbar' (*Scottish Naturalist*, 1935 (212):50. Thorburn's last published material and one of his few contributions to a scientific journal.)

Trevor-Battye, Aubyn. 'Archibald Thorburn and his work' (*The Artist* (London) 20(211) July 1897, 318–330. Contains seventeen monochrome reproductions of Thorburn's drawings and paintings ranging from the spitting fury of a 'Scottish Wild Cat' to a study of 'Dead Blue Hares'. Also, in the August number of the magazine, as a tail-piece to an article on page 389, there are two studies of male blackcap, one of which appears to have been printed 'on its side'. In the July number, and immediately preceding the article on Thorburn, is an illustrated article on his contemporary Bruno Liljefors, entitled 'A Prince of Animal Painters'.)

Trevor-Battye, Aubyn (editor). *Lord Lilford on Birds* . . . (Hutchinson & Co, London, 1903, 312pp. Contains thirteen monochrome plates by Thorburn, including a portrait of Lord Lilford in his study.)

Turner, W. J. (editor). *Nature in Britain* (Collins, London, 1946, 324pp. Britain in Pictures Guinea volume, has most, though not all, of the Thorburn plates which appear in the BIP books dealing with 'Wild Life' and 'Birds' [see **Fraser-Darling** and **Fisher**].)

Vandervell, Anthony and **Coles**, Charles. *Game and the English Landscape* (Debrett's Peerage Ltd, London, 1980, 159pp. Has colour reproductions of two plates from *British Birds* (1915–18) much reduced in size.)

Verner, Col W. W. C. *My Life Among the Wild Birds of Spain* (John Bale, Sons and Danielsson Ltd, London, 1909, 468pp. Contains numerous monochrome illustrations of which 16 are by Thorburn, being 11 from 'Lilford' and 5 from 'Irby' (2nd edn). Thorburn's name has been erased from all 16 plates.)

Vesey-Fitzgerald, Brian. *British Game*. (Collins, London, 1946, 239pp. Has two colour plates, being reproduced from Millais . . . *Game Birds*, and showing ptarmigan and quail.)

Watson, Alfred E. T. *King Edward VII as a Sportsman* (Longmans, Green & Co, London, 1911, 381pp. Decorative boards. Contains ten coloured plates, of which seven are by Thorburn; these depicting: pheasant, wild duck, partridge, Edward VII shooting, park-deer, grouse and wild deer.)

Watson, Alfred E. T. (editor). *The Badminton Magazine of Sports and Pastimes*. (Heinemann, London.) There follows a chronological list of articles contained in this magazine which have been illustrated by Thorburn, together with details of author, etc.

AUGUST 1895 'A North Derbyshire Moor' by the Marquess of Granby, MP (3 monochrome plates by Thorburn).

SEPTEMBER 1895 'Partridge Shooting' by Lord Walsingham (3 monochrome plates by Thorburn).

OCTOBER 1895 'Highland Sport in the Last Generation' by Alexander Innes-Shand (12 Thorburn monochromes).

NOVEMBER 1895 'The Shot-gun in Norway' by Sir Henry Pottinger, Bt (5 Thorburn monochrome plates).

DECEMBER 1895 'The Big Stag of Beinn Nan Nighean' by Sir Herbert Maxwell, Bt, MP (2 monochrome plates by Thorburn).

JANUARY 1896 'A Difficult Shoot' by H. P. Mules (1 Thorburn monochrome).

MARCH 1896 'The Rifle in Norway' by Sir Henry Pottinger, Bt (1 monochrome by Thorburn).

APRIL 1896 'Some Poachers' by Alexander Innes-Shand (4 Thorburn monochromes).

MAY 1896 'Deer Hawking in India' by Col H. Ward, CIE (8 monochromes by Thorburn (Goshawks)).

AUGUST 1896 'The Grouse' by Alexander Innes-Shand (3 Thorburn monochromes).

SEPTEMBER 1896 'The Little Brown Bird (The common partridge)' by the Marquess of Granby (3 monochromes by Thorburn).

OCTOBER 1896 'The Pheasants' by Alexander Innes-Shand (2 Thorburn monochromes).

NOVEMBER 1896 'Sport in the Channel Islands' by H. Heron (1 monoplate by Thorburn).

JANUARY 1897 'The Coverts' by Alexander Innes-Shand (3 Thorburn monochromes).

FEBRUARY 1897 'A Pheasant Farm' by Major Charles J. Boyle (1 monochrome by Thorburn).

NOVEMBER 1897 'Reminiscences of a Pheasant' by Hon. John Scott-Montague, MP (12 Thorburn monochrome plates).

JANUARY to JUNE 1900 being volume X (The sepia frontispiece to this volume is by Thorburn and shows partridges in flight as – 'Over the Stubble Fields'. This volume also contains some nice work by J. G. Keulemans).

In compiling the above list of Thorburn's work I have endeavoured to be as thorough as possible, though in the area of 'Private Publications' which are often difficult to research, I acknowledge that there may well be some omissions. I trust that any such omissions will be pardoned.

GARRY M. BATTEN
1986

Chronology

1860 31 May	Archibald Thorburn born at Lasswade near Edinburgh.
1872	Already talented at art, illustrating church hymn cards for the services at his local church.
1880	First entry to Summer Exhibition of Royal Academy. Accepted. See Appendix of Royal Academy pictures.
1882	His first published illustrations of birds appeared, in J. E. Harting's *Sketches of Bird Life*. See Appendix.
1883	His first coloured illustrations of birds appeared in W. Swaysland's *Familiar Wild Birds*. See Appendix.
1885	Moved to London – 25 Stanley Gardens NW.
1887–1898	Working on the 268 watercolours for Lord Lilford's monumental work *Coloured Figures of the Birds of the British Islands*. See Appendix.
1889	First visited Gaick. Saw and drew his first red deer and ptarmigan there.
1891	Moved to 88 Fellows Road in London.
1896	Appointed A. Baird-Carter of 61 Jermyn Street SW1 his agent.
1896 23 Sept	Married Constance Mudie – whose father Charles Edward had founded the famous Mudie Lending Library.
1898	Elected a Fellow of the Zoological Society.
1899	Painted the first Christmas Card for the RSPB – roseate terns.
1900	His last entry for the Royal Academy. See Appendix.
1902	His agent Baird-Carter moved to larger premises in Jermyn Street, vacating No 61 and moving to No 70.
1902	Thorburn and his wife moved to High Leybourne at Hascombe, near Godalming where he lived for the rest of his life.
1910–11	These two years saw a remarkable output of large and very fine quality pictures of gamebirds before he began work on his forthcoming *British Birds* of 1915–16, involving writing the text as well as painting 82 watercolours.
1915–16	First book both written and illustrated by Thorburn appeared. *British Birds* 4 vols, quarto, together with a supplement. See Appendix.
1919	Baird-Carter died and was succeeded by W. F. Embleton as Thorburn's agent at No 70 Jermyn Street. Embleton had been both apprentice and assistant to Baird-Carter.
1919	Publication of his *A Naturalist's Sketch Book*. See Appendix.
1920	Publication of his *British Mammals* in two volumes with 50 plates. See Appendix.
1921	Another marvellous year for a spate of very high quality imperial size watercolours of gamebirds, wildfowl, eagles etc.
1922	Painted the plates of *Gamebirds and Wildfowl of Great Britain and Ireland*. See Appendix.
1923	Published his *Gamebirds and Wildfowl of Great Britain and Ireland* with 30 plates.
1925	Publication of his *British Birds* 4 vols, octavo, 192 plates.
1926	Thorburn's great friend and patron J. Henry Dixon died with whom he had stayed on many painting expeditions to the Highlands of Scotland
1927	Elected vice-president RSPB
1930	Thorburn underwent a major operation for cancer.
1931–5	His condition steadily deteriorated.
1934	Last signed print issued – Blackgame in winter.
1935	Painted his last Christmas card for the RSPB of a goldcrest.
1935 9 Oct	Thorburn died.
1935 13 Oct	Thorburn buried in Busbridge churchyard nr. Godalming.

Iceland Falcon and Greenland Falcon
Watercolour 9¾ × 6¾in and 9½ × 6½in respectively
Original watercolours for plates 16 and 18 respectively, vol 1 of *Coloured Figures of the Birds of the British Islands* by Lord Lilford, 1885–98

Some of the most exquisite watercolours of birds ever painted must surely be the 268 carefully finished works carried out by the young Mr Thorburn on commission to Lord Lilford of Northampton for his monumental work *Coloured Figures of the Birds of the British Islands*, published in thirty-six parts 1885–98 and subsequently bound in seven volumes.

We include in this book two typical examples from this work of the young man's breathtaking ability and output, 'The Iceland Falcon' and 'The Greenland Falcon'.

Thorburn spent much time at Lilford Hall, ancestral home of his lordship, during the ten years the commission took to complete, spending countless hours in the elaborate and extensive aviaries there, the pride and joy of Lord Lilford, in which very many exotic birds were successfully kept and reared. It would be here that Thorburn drew his first sketches from life of these noble, splendid birds, referring to skins perhaps (also at Lilford Hall) for intricate plumage detail and to a variety of material from which to construct painstakingly accurate renderings of the wilderness environment in which the birds live.

For a young man in his twenties the achievements are remarkable. Beautifully drawn, the birds are soft of texture yet round and solid of form, exuding majesty with the characteristic aggressive alertness of both species.

Already Thorburn is an expert with shadow, quickly using it to block in areas of the distant hills, shaping them as he goes. Notice his unobtrusive use of shadow to gently curl and lift the feathers away from the slab of rock on which they lie uneasily – a sure and often repeated Thorburn touch of observation and realism.

Just occasionally, as a very young man, Thorburn 'copied' a work by his idol Joseph Wolf, a kindly and helpful old man who was, in Thorburn's view, the finest draughtsman of birds of all time. Thorburn took lessons from him, regularly visiting his studio on Primrose Hill and missed his advice and help greatly when he died in 1899.

Unlike some artists that come to mind, if he did copy a picture Thorburn always inscribed it accordingly, completing the work with a clear conscience. Here, with the Iceland falcon, although the work is in every brushful Thorburn and not Wolf, he generously withdraws into the shadows by granting Wolf his full name whilst recording his own very considerable involvement in the work by merely adding his initials – A.T.

Many pictures of Iceland and Greenland falcons have been painted since Thorburn but, in my opinion, he alone captured their grandeur and sleek aggressiveness like no other.

A.T. after J. Wolf

A.Thorburn

The Fallen Beech

Oils 14 × 21in, signed and dated 1886
Pheasants feeding in a wood

Painted at the age of twenty-six, this picture represents one of the few oil paintings by Thorburn, for he painted predominantly in watercolour, much preferring the medium with which to capture the softness of a bird's plumage or a creature's fur or hair.

However, he was, as seen here, a highly accomplished oil painter, this particular example adequately confirming this viewpoint, even though he was still a relatively young man.

Behind a fallen beech trunk, a cock and three hen pheasants quietly feed and laze. Upon the woodland floor they pick their way, alert lest an intruder should encroach upon their haven.

The picture is well balanced and composed, faithfully depicting such a scene without sentimental exaggeration yet remaining generous in items of interest to absorb the viewing eye. The upturned wasp and fallen leaves, the sunlit bracken twinkling from beneath the tree, the work skilfully lifted by the lovely blue sky escape route from the otherwise overpowering confines of the situation.

Again the construction of the painting securely blocks in the distance element for the viewer, the fallen tree expertly leading our eye into the picture. Framed against the upright tree standing in the centre of the canvas and that in turn framed against those in the middle distance, one is able to walk with the pheasants into the clearing beyond.

On innumerable occasions Thorburn positioned his birds in an overlapping constructional form and here the three on the left of the work effectively take different block positions within the depth of the painting.

Highlighting, shadow and attention to detail – all hallmarks of Thorburn's work – are already abundantly evident in this work, although the artist is not yet thirty.

Detail This particular detail illustrates so well Thorburn's obvious flair and ease as an oil painter. Although he himself found oils much more difficult and unpredictable than watercolour, there is no sign of hesitation or incompetence here. Instead an assuredness of this young hand often not shown in the work of others much older.

Notice the angle of the eye affecting the features of the bird, as the hen pheasant is slightly alarmed and apprehensive at the prospect of dealing with the whirring wasp. How well he portrays that intensity.

Such attention to the detail of nature's story as a whole sets Thorburn apart from others who more often than not omit such mundane accuracies, devoting their time to detailing and delineating every feather of each poor bird in their attempt to capture realism.

With accomplished handling of shadow he expertly moulds the bird's shape and form, capturing the nape of the neck so well, rounding its back and creating space beneath the bird's long tail.

Propped on shadow, the leaves curl casually away from the woodland floor and even the wasp is not forgotten as, with merest touch, its shape is assured.

A. Thorburn.

The King of Birds
Watercolour 29½ × 21¼in, signed and dated 1899
A pair of golden eagles in the Highlands

Many of Thorburn's early compositions leading up to and just after the turn of the century were often constructed by drawing the birds large in the landscape. Many of his flying gamebirds up to this period in his life followed this pattern, often resembling 'bombers' swooping low over the countryside.

This particular picture nicely demonstrates this early technique, with the main bird consuming at least a quarter of the total paper area. Comparing this with a similar subject composed on the same size of paper 'The Home of the Golden Eagle' of some thirty years later, will immediately demonstrate the difference, the birds now drawn much smaller in the landscape, resulting in a generally more overall pleasing composition and picture.

Although large and broadly painted, the main bird here is beautifully handled, exuding aggression and majesty in plenty and full of shape and shadow. Impeccably balanced, it would be difficult to better the eyes, feet and beak, although Thorburn throughout his life invariably excelled at such things that others found so difficult. The loosely painted background, whilst truthfully depicting the wild environment of the bird, perfectly complements the more detailed drama within the bird itself.

Some years ago the background of this picture was quite seriously damaged in a house fire but, thankfully, has been expertly and perfectly restored. The picture was very kindly donated to the Museum by a West-country clergyman.

Notice again 'The Home of the Golden Eagle' on p48. Although painted rather more quickly with a greater reliance being placed upon washes with which to skilfully form and feather the birds, Thorburn's unfaltering care and attention to detail survives the passage of thirty years, as he continues to portray the eyes and feet with such lifelike, masterly conviction.

Surprise
Watercolour 4¾ × 6½in, unsigned
A meeting between rabbits and a cock bullfinch

Thorburn was barely twenty years of age when he produced this charming little study. At this time in his life he was much influenced by the work of Joseph Wolf, a kindly and helpful man who lived in St John's Wood. He was a remarkable draughtsman and a very distinguished wildlife artist of the time, from whom the young Thorburn took lessons, Thorburn greatly respecting his skills. Indeed many years later Thorburn, and his great friend and contemporary George Lodge, often remarked that Wolf was the best draughtsman of them all.

This watercolour is much in the manner of Wolf, not only in overall composition and careful watercolour control but also in the somewhat sentimental stance to its composition and more delicate colouring.

Although unsigned and undated, it has all the promise of the great things yet to come from the young hand that painted it and is a constant source of pleasure to all who look upon it. Again observe Thorburn's ability to play upon one base colour, gently exhausting all its hues and tones.

Sunrise over Gaick
Watercolour 21¼ × 29½in, signed and dated 1904
Ptarmigan awakening on the winter snows

Gaick in Inverness-shire is a wild and remote place. The 25,000 acre estate ranges from ridge across corrie from scree to glen and back again. Winter's snowy mantle gives the place an even bleaker air where, on the highest tops, the ptarmigan eke out their meagre existence from the vast white wilderness that stretches as far as the eye can see.

Thorburn first went there in 1889 when he saw and sketched his first living ptarmigan. Thereafter he returned regularly, filling his sketch books with drawings of deer and grouse, hare and eagles, as well as ptarmigan.

This particularly lovely picture shows these particularly lovely birds at sunrise. Thorburn, warmly clad and out on the hill before dawn, was in position with pencil and sketch book as the first light of the brief winter's day coaxed back to life the pack of birds, slowly awakening from their slumbers amid the snow and ice-clad landscape. One group of birds, feeling the first touch of warmth, begin to preen and feed and fly, whilst those still in the ice-cold shadows, unmoving, slumber on awhile.

White upon white upon white was the challenge Thorburn set himself. What a challenge for a painter, expecially in watercolour. But, dissecting the picture, that is indeed its construction; white birds shown upon white snow, the whole painted upon white paper. Revelling in the challenge, Thorburn exhausted all the plays of light upon the winter scene. Notice how the grey-green herbage is reflected upon the snow and then reflected upon the birds, their snow-white plumage being overlaid by a grey-green wash by this acutely observant and highly accomplished artist naturalist.

The birds, many being drawn in the most difficult of foreshortened positions, are neatly overlaid, one afront of the next thereby using the space of the painting to great advantage.

Notice the delightfully unobtrusive yet firm compositional hand that guides us through the picture. Beginning with the main bird bottom-left and the main birds bottom-right, the eye centres on the cluster of birds in the middle of the page before drifting right to the flying birds and onwards to the pointed hilltop of Gaick highlighted by the early morning sun.

Detail Thorburn loved ptarmigan, being captivated by both them, with their ever-changing seasonal plumage variations, and the wilderness of their high and lonely habitat.

Winter brings an even greater desolation to such places and Thorburn marvelled at the courage and endurance of such small-seeming bundles of snow-white feathers that eked out their existence in these austere and inhospitable surroundings.

He spent many hours, chilled to the bone, sketching such scenes at sunrise and sundown, his hands nimbled by warm mittens, recording the birds themselves with their postures and habitats as well as detailing their haunt, fascinated by the play of light upon the slopes of snow.

During his lifetime Thorburn produced a considerable number of very fine pictures of these birds in winter, yet never is the same composition seen twice. Although the same situation is depicted, the component birds used in the formation of each vary beautifully; the artist has carefully selected drawings from his numerous sketch books that form both a pleasing and accurate composition, and he has at the same time given the works a freshness and individuality all of their own.

Just such a variation is seen on p93, 'Ptarmigan at Sunrise', where, although both works show ptarmigan at Gaick in winter, each retains its own personal charm and appeal.

Gleaning after the Shooters

Watercolour 29 × 21in, signed and dated 1906
A fox approaches a pheasant lying dead upon the snow

A pheasant, not destined for the larder, lies cold and stiff upon the wintry ground, the few feathers and specks of blood adding to the finality of its life. The hungry fox, catching the taint upon the wind, approaches with much caution lest its own seeming good fortune should prove to be its untimely downfall and death as well.

A lovely example of a narrative painting. Something has happened, something else is just about to happen. The story continues but must be unravelled for ourselves.

The picture is constructed on a series of diagonals, one's eye being led from the dead bird's head along its body to the tip of its tail and then, anti-clockwise, around the top of the page, following now the line of the fox which, in turn, returns our eye to the pheasant.

Throughout the work there is a co-ordination of colour, the same colours progressing as well as being re-worked. Thorburn pioneered this sort of treatment of the subject and has not been followed since, most artists preferring to straddle the entire palette rather than to major on the colour harmony of one or two pigments as Thorburn often did.

Again one senses the presence of man but does not see him and unlike many painters of foxes who depict them wild and ruthless, the timidity of the beast is beautifully captured as it edges out from cover.

Thorburn, the careful observer of how nature functions, displays his own very personal craft so unlike the purely illustrative approach employed by the vast majority of bird and animal painters both before and since his time. Notice the rippling movement of muscle, tense with nervousness, of the fox and compare that with the solid, unmoving stiffness of the dead bird. How well he captures life and death within the countryside upon the selfsame page.

Disputed Rights

Oil 43½ × 64in, signed and dated 1901
Two red deer stags locked in battle

One almost hears the snorting and gasping of the two stags locked in combat in this remarkably intense work, painted when Thorburn was forty-one years of age. It represents an extremely fine example of his skill as an oil painter. Oil paintings by Thorburn are rare and he often remarked how he found them an infinitely more difficult medium with which to capture the softness of fur, feather or hair than watercolour. Here however, from the rendering of the hair on the beasts in battle and from the foliage of the foreground to the delicacy of the distant hills, all are superbly handled.

Totally devoid of the sentimentality that so often accompanied paintings of birds and animals at that time, the stags really are locked in a very real and fervent dispute, wide-eyed and snorting, perspiring and intense, whilst the hinds on the other hand, remain silent though alert, melting into the mist-laden background, patiently awaiting the eventual outcome of the challenge.

The play of light and shade upon the banks and over and beneath the fighting beasts is most successful. Such an accomplishment as this, amongst others, places Thorburn alongside the best of the oil painters of the period, whatever their subject and in spite of the difficulties of which he spoke when painting in this medium compared with his much preferred watercolour.

The composition is most satisfying, pinpointing our eyes initially as it does upon the heads of the grappling beasts and then allowing us a gentle exploration of their bodies before quite quickly leading us up to the waiting hinds in the central background who in turn point to our escape in the break in the clouds beyond.

Lost in the Glen

Watercolour 27¼ × 45¼in, signed and dated 1897

A wounded stag has died, attracting the eagles by its taint in the wind

Tracking down the carcase of a recently shot red deer whilst out on the hills at Gaick, Thorburn made a number of detailed sketches of the unfortunate creature as it lay across the ice-cold slab of rock that winter's day, carefully noting the hills beyond and the vegetation in the foreground. Had he had access to carbon paper in those days I feel sure he would have used it. As it was he made perhaps three or four virtually identical sketches and then retreated, tucking himself away behind a boulder to await the arrival of the eagles, beckoned to the spot by the taint upon the wind. Now, as the bird pitched upon the carcase first facing the artist and then turning to fend off its approaching mate, Thorburn quickly drew in the various positions and attitudes of the bird (as well as noting the one gliding in the background) upon his already prepared sketches of the unmoving scene.

This huge watercolour is a superlative piece of work, capturing so well the death and desolation of the moment. The thirty-seven-year-old artist excels himself with the composition of the picture, one's eye being positively yet discreetly led up from the righthand bottom corner along the line of the stag, to the mighty eagle upon its back and then on to the distant, gliding bird which in turn leads to the wilderness beyond. Upon analysis one perceives that guidance through the picture is brilliantly achieved by a progression of tonal changes of one base colour.

The picture abounds in narrative, though needing to be carefully unwrapped – the bullet mark set well back from the heart, indicating the animal was wounded and not killed outright, leaving the beast to stagger away, finally collapsing and dying slumped across the granite slab as shown.

Thorburn's bold use of shadow springs the stag's limp leg away from the rock as well as lifting the body of the eagle clearly above the back of the unfortunate beast. The painting in watercolour of the dead eye is the work of a great technician. Compare it with the very living eye of the eagle.

Again one senses the presence of man the hunter. The death and debris caused by him is carefully recorded for all to see, thus freeing the eagles from the accusing finger.

Detail A casual glance at this detail may well remind us of the large and spectacular hunting scenes, both French and English, of that era or a little before. But, taking a closer look, it is easy to appreciate the total omission of the sentimentality that normally surrounded such works.

The realism of the situation is startling. How well Thorburn captured death – both in the ice-blue eye of the unfortunate beast and the downward angle of the collapsed neck which accentuates and confirms the fatality. Crumpled in this position, one also clearly senses the dead weight of the beast.

Again can be seen the artist exploiting hues and tints from within one base colour, flavouring both beast and background with this lovely yet difficult technique.

Notice how expertly he lifts the ear of the stag clear of the brown background, shaping it, and the head generally, with fluent graded applications of shadow.

As a final confirmation of death, Thorburn attracts attention to the once warm blood now firmly congealed upon the snow.

Archibald Thorburn
1897

Redstarts

Watercolour $10\frac{1}{2} \times 7\frac{1}{4}$in, signed and dated 1917

Cock and hen redstart in a woodland glade

The deep velvet tones of the lush woodland background, broken only by the highlighting of nearby leaves of ivy, form both a pleasing yet accurate backcloth to the picture, contrasting with the vivid red, black and white of this most lovely of woodland birds, the cock redstart.

Flowed on wet and free, the colours mingle harmoniously, the unseen hand controlling the task with great flair and conviction. The rotting tree stump in the foreground, on which the birds briefly perch, again creates a pleasing contrast to the rich boldness of the woodland beyond, positioning the birds close to us.

One almost sees the characteristic quiver of the red tail of the cock bird as Thorburn lifts it clear of the tree by confident placing of deep shadow. The hen bird, attired in more sombre hues, blends with branch and bough amid the woodland glade, not to be easily seen whilst upon her nest or with her young.

This charming watercolour is a good example of a typical, almost mundane commission for the artist by this period in his life. Taking little or no more than a day to complete, it overflows with the quality of execution and individuality of touch that was to be so consistent throughout Thorburn's life. Commissions would tumble through his letter box almost daily requesting perhaps a pair of robins, a red grouse, stag, or wild cat. Remarkably all would be of a consistent quality, similar to the particular commission shown here calling for a pair of redstarts. Even in a small everyday picture, Thorburn allows us an escape from the confines and intricacies of the scene, guiding us to the top lefthand corner and the blue sky beyond.

The Covey at Daybreak

Watercolour 27 × 45in, signed and dated 1892

A covey of partridge awakens upon the dew-damp stubble of autumn

Three drops of dew lying uneasily upon the blackberry leaves confirm the break of day. A partridge covey awakens upon the autumn stubble, the old cock bird rasping out his grating greeting to the sunrise far beyond the hillside brow. Meanwhile, another covey glides in from a neighbouring field upon which they have spent the autumnal night. In the valley below a farmstead nestles snugly within its patchworked pastures, the harvest safely gathered in amid the barnyard ricks.

The picture is indeed a history lesson. Standing by should be a man in a smock, sharpening his scythe, for that's how long ago it was painted. The unevenly cut straw stalks retell of days long before the combine harvester, even indeed before the horse-drawn binder. The blackberries, sprawling out from unkempt hedgerow into the adjoining corn fields have also long since gone, persecuted by exuberant knapsack sprayer and over-efficient farmer. With the disappearance of these very English things so common long ago, the English partridge have all but vanished too.

Again Thorburn awakens our senses, causing us to hear the cock crowing and the dog barking as the first light of day arouses the farmstead below. He cleverly places the cock bird's head against the morning light, emphasising both the time of day and the principal subject of the picture at the same time. Imagine how the head would have been lost and much impact erased had the head been placed against the purple grey of the receding cloud.

The solid, three-dimensional shape of the birds is extremely successful, so different from the flat, lifeless maps of birds' plumages that sadly one so often sees in modern bird portraiture. How cleverly Thorburn puts in the degrees of distance, the beautifully painted broken ears of barley on the lefthand side of the picture emphasising the less distinct corn beyond. As seen in so much of Thorburn's work, note his clever unobtrusive use of the autumnal palette of browns and golds, coaxing as he does every shade and hue from within its repertoire.

Partridges awakening upon the stubble always intrigued Thorburn and this very early depiction of the scene – painted when he was thirty-two – forms an interesting companion to 'A Frosty Dawn' shown on p85, painted a third of a century later.

In his early work the artist's tightly controlled, carefully painted approach to the subject can be seen, with each aspect receiving considerable care and attention. In 'A Frosty Dawn', however, a much less restrained technique is used, the whole picture fluent and free, bubbling over with a confidence that ensues from experience and success, as the artist flows on the background with great speed and compulsion.

A. Thorburn
1892

Blackcock Fighting

Watercolour 14½ × 21in, signed and dated 1901

Two male black grouse spar at their lek on a Scottish hillside

The silence of the dawn, advancing slowly across a Scottish hillside, is broken by the buffeting of blackcock at the lek. Two males display and spar, watched over by a nearby female, or greyhen as she is called. Another male, perhaps attracted by the dispute, drifts in from an adjoining hillside hollow to stake his particular claim with the ladies of the morning.

Thorburn loved blackgame, the collective name for the male and female of this fast-dwindling species, much enjoying the challenge of capturing, as he does so beautifully here, the blue sheen upon the birds' black feathers.

Their haunt, too, amid the heathery hollows, sprinkled here and there with clumps of silver birch, was a particular favourite of his and one he never tired of visiting, sketching and featuring in his finished pictures.

The birds, exquisitely drawn and painted, stand well, the deep shadows successfully lifting them away from the background. And the delicate washes, expertly placed and controlled, capture so well the stillness of the early morning on a lonely Scottish hillside.

Detail In this enlargement of the heads of the blackcock buffeting at dawn is clearly seen Thorburn's technique of constructing a bird out of paint.

Constantly viewers of his work remark upon his painstaking detail. However, here can be seen quite clearly that he brilliantly implied such detail but rarely incorporated it.

Analyse the building of a bird technique he employed upon the righthand blackcock. Note the broad bands of colour placed in quickly and with much confidence. The initial tonal washes are then steadily added to by increasingly darker ones, culminating in the application of black to firmly and positively mould the shape into the bird.

Thorburn's rare yet undeniable skill was knowing exactly where and how far to place each grade of colour, almost magically transforming an initially flat outline into a living, breathing three-dimensional creature as one watched. Final streaking in of a darker colour – always though at exactly the correct angle – was all that was necessary to complete the bird, implying to the viewer many hours of detail painting.

Observe, too, the subtleties of the palette used in the picture, where the blues and reds and pinks of the birds spill over into the background almost unnoticed though very much intentional, as a perfect balance and blend to the overall pleasing effect of the painting.

Archibald Thorburn
1901

The Home of the Golden Eagle

Watercolour 29 × 20¾in, signed and dated 1927

A pair of golden eagles at their eyrie high on a Scottish hillside

High on a rocky precipice the golden eagles have their eyrie. Chiselled in upon a ledge, the huge nest of sticks and dead heather rests upon a bed of bracken, thus lifting the young away from the damp below, keeping their home well drained in time of storm and torrent. One parent stands guard, awaiting the hare its mate has just brought home. This it will tear into swallowable shreds for the eyasses, whilst the hunter turns and, slipping away from the ledge, quickly sails off in search of another tasty morsel for the ever-hungry young.

On discovering this particular eyrie in the Scottish Highlands in 1919, Thorburn made innumerable sketches there over a period of several days, spending many hours waiting crouched, cramped and cold with spyglass, sketch book and pencil.

During the years that followed he then produced several major pictures from this original material, all nicely varied yet united by the common thread of the same huge nest on the high rock face with the loch below.

With unerring skill, Thorburn quickly shapes the birds by bold use of shadow, lifting the throat of the bird at the top positively away from its back and, with the merest flick of chestnut, shaping the head of the bird below. With shadow and shading skilfully applied, what at first may appear a flat, lifeless map of a bird and its plumage can so quickly be transformed into a round and solid, living creature as he so ably shows here.

Whilst the mountain hare obviously features prominently on the golden eagle's menu, telltale clues of other tasty morsels litter the spot as scattered feathers of ptarmigan and red grouse lie uneasily upon the wind.

Comparing this work with another very fine picture of golden eagles of similar size and format shown on p36 'The King of Birds', the difference can be noticed in Thorburn's approach to the same subject some thirty years later. In his earlier work often his birds were drawn large, consuming perhaps as much as half the surface area with one image. Later on, however, as seen here, the images were drawn in much smaller, allowing room for considerably more habitat and narrative to be incorporated in the composition. The usual result of this was to create a more overall satisfying version of a very similar scene and situation.

The Shadow of Death

Watercolour 23½ × 35½in, signed and dated 1893

Ptarmigan in winter crouch as they watch a golden eagle sail by high overhead

The shadow of a golden eagle, effortlessly riding the thermals, drifts along an ice-gripped ridge. The huge bird, intent upon securing sustenance in such hard times, scours the countryside for hare or ptarmigan, both camouflaged in white attire against just such an eagle's eye. Journeying mile after mile over snowbound corrie and glen, the bird glides past a pack of ptarmigan, crouching well nigh motionless high on the hill, quietly waiting for the danger to pass. Sprinkled like snowflakes upon a patch of snow-free ground, they preen and feed upon the meagre fare such high and inhospitable places provide.

Painted at Gaick in Inverness-shire on the first of the many occasions Thorburn was to stay at this splendid 25,000 acre Highland estate, the background, freely painted and with great confidence, depicts the pointed hilltop that Thorburn invariably incorporated in a composition originating at Gaick. The ptarmigan themselves – twenty-four in all – contrast with the broad painting of the mountains and glen, being round and firm, solid and convincingly shaped living creatures, nonstereotyped, each intent upon its own particular need or inclination of the moment.

Thorburn painted this picture at the age of thirty-nine and it is typical of his large, carefully composed, painstakingly accurate yet marvellously pleasing pictures of gamebirds that have so prominently set him worlds apart from others in this field, before or since.

A.Thorburn

The Lost Stag

Watercolour 29½ × 45¼in, signed and dated 1899

Exhibited Royal Academy 1899 Exhibition No 1128

Thorburn had some twenty-one pictures exhibited at the Royal Academy, all between the years of 1880 to 1900. His first, entitled 'The Moor', which he entered and had accepted at the early age of twenty, depicted red grouse whilst his last, painted and shown in 1900, was of golden eagles. Other subjects he chose to enter during this twenty-year period included red deer, blackgame, pheasant and partridge.

His penultimate entry of 1899, shown here, combined both eagles and deer in the dramatic composition 'The Lost Stag'.

A taint on the wind, whilst spelling misfortune for one brings fortune for another. A golden eagle, scouring corrie and glen in search of food, is guided to the carcase of a luckless stag and, with glaring eye, quickly stakes its claim, voicing a warning to any who might challenge his prize.

Broadly and boldly painted, the bright greens of the foreground remain as fresh today as when painted almost a hundred years ago, tribute indeed to the quality of Winsor & Newton paints that Thorburn used throughout his lifetime. The overall broad treatment of the scene is confidently and compellingly transformed by the numerous bold bands of shadow solidly applied to beast and bird with great effect. The background ridge, engulfed in a mass of swirling mists, effectively achieves an escape through the glen and far beyond.

The comparison between the eye of the living and that of the dead is achieved with great distinction, as is the foreshortening of the massive hooked beak of the bird, correctly casting a shadow across its left eye which in turn twists the head out of the page and away from the slab of rock behind.

Detail In Britain, the eagle and the stag fear but one predator, namely man. How well they both blend with the background thus confusing the searching eye of the hunter.

In this huge and compelling Royal Academy watercolour, Thorburn excels at composing a rich harmony of hues and tones from a very limited base palette. The brown, golds and mauves spill over from beast and bird to background and back again. Note how the mauves of the great bird's drooped wing flow over onto the hindquarters of the dead stag, Thorburn distinctly differentiating between the two by lighter streaks of colour and angle of deft detail.

This detail clearly shows an outstanding example of shadow painting as, knowingly, Thorburn confidently lays in areas of darker tones, twisting and shaping the neck at the same time positioning it comfortably behind the shoulder of the wing. Notice how the scapular feathers across the back of the eagle are lightly lifted with such confidence and success by boldly painting in lines of shadow.

The strength and ferocity of the bird are ably applied with paint upon paper, with remarkable portrayals of eye, beak and foot.

Archibald Thorburn
899

Eagle Owl

Watercolour 11 × 7¼in, signed and dated 1917
An eagle owl prepares for an evening's hunting

An eagle owl, sensing the chill of the dusk edging its way through the forest, slips silently from its daytime den. Momentarily it sits upon a promontory, quietly surveying the fir-clad hillside, before embarking upon yet another night of hunting.

Thorburn, now fifty-seven years of age, is regularly producing a finished watercolour of this quality and size almost daily. The original pencil sketch taken from life may well have been made years earlier, at Regent's Park Zoo perhaps, or earlier still at Lilford Hall, and then, in response to a commission, redrawn and placed in a landscape of local Surrey forest that Thorburn knew so well.

Invariably his finished pictures were constructed in this way, with each aspect, bird, beast, rock or reed being lifted from an appropriate original sketch book and skilfully redrawn and positioned upon the page, forming an accurate yet overall pleasing composition. Such faithfulness to nature in all her aspects and moods is unquestionably one of the prime reasons for the continuing freshness and success of Thorburn's pictures.

Here again we see Thorburn's skill at portraying the sense of the unknown, as we imagine the rabbit and vole and other creatures of the dusk upon which the owl will prey, and yet do not see them.

One eye shadowed by the forehead and protruding beak and crisp shadows beneath the bird's tactile talons, confirm Thorburn's unerring knowledge of his subject and attention to detail.

Morning

Oils 27½ × 45in, signed and dated 1901
Red grouse awakening on the Scottish moors

Thorburn painted rarely in oils, much preferring watercolour with which to capture the softness and delicacy of birds' feathers or creatures' hair or fur.

It was in his early, formative years, that a number of oils were completed beginning in the early 1880s and quickly petering out soon after the turn of the century, becoming virtually non existent after 1905.

This lovely example of his skills with oil paints is very much handled in the grand manner of the Victorian landscape and animal painters, to a degree reminiscent of Landseer though without the sentimental cosiness that shrouded much of his work. It also recalls for us the tradition of the English romantics such as Richard Wilson and Joseph Wright of Derby.

It seems strange that for someone who was so accomplished and painted with such an assured hand that more pictures in this medium did not follow these remarkable early efforts. For one who painted so infrequently in oils the results are quite outstanding.

The picture records a breathtakingly lovely dawn breaking over the Scottish Highlands. The early light illuminates the banks of mist still trapped in the gullies, soon to be steadily wiped away by the gradually warming rays of the sun. Here, as with practically all his Scottish scenes, Thorburn captures the immenseness of the Highlands, showing nature in all her glory.

Note the remarkable composition upon two strong diagonals, from bottom-left to top-right and from bottom-right to mid-left, each centring the principal red grouse, expertly leaving the bird's head to protrude effectively yet unobtrusively against the sky.

Thorburn's sunrise paintings invariably place the head of the principal bird against the brightening dawn, cleverly yet discreetly emphasising both the main subject of the picture and the time of day simultaneously. A similar example of this technique can be seen on p79 in 'The Morning Call'.

Thorburn regularly used this unobtrusive yet important component of picture building throughout his life, where examples from long before the turn of the century can be seen, such as 'The Covey at Daybreak' on p45, and others drawn only a matter of years before his death, for example 'A Frosty Dawn' on p85.

Mountain Hare and Irish Hare
Watercolour 12 × 15¼in, signed and dated 1919
Original watercolour for Thorburn's *British Mammals*, 1920, Vol 2, plate 34

Thorburn painted mammals with equal ease and accomplishment as he did birds. In fact, it is doubtful whether the illustrations he produced for his book *British Mammals*, published in 1920, have ever been equalled let alone surpassed. Each is a gem in its own right, whether whale or weasel, bat or badger, all so impeccably drawn and accurate in bodily detail, stance and attitude. But more than that, each is set amongst a beautifully composed and painted piece of habitat, invariably decorated with bloom or butterfly perhaps, adding both charm and accuracy to the work.

The mountain hare sits atop a rocky outcrop, acutely alert for golden eagle scouring the wilderness for just such a tasty morsel. So convincingly alive and intent is the beast that one almost sees its whiskers twitching as the creature assimilates the scents upon the wind.

With bold shadows Thorburn quickly lifts the ear clear of the animal's back and the fuzzed edge of its back and chest gives it real 'roundness' and form.

The handling of the sky is quite exquisite. Painted on pale green paper, the blue wash is dealt with so expertly that one seeks yet does not find its edge, as the colour intensifies towards the centre of the page. A deft hand at creating distance in a picture, Thorburn paints in the whitened twig across the lower back as he nears completion of the work, hanging space between it and the fur of the beast with great skill.

Detail It is doubtful whether anyone captured the character of a hare in watercolour better than we see Thorburn doing here.

So well does he instil into the picture the alertness of eye and the overpowering awareness of the creature, silently dissecting the wind for the faintest taint or echo borne upon it.

Early on in his career Thorburn had perfected a technique with which to denote fur or hair, often such a solid dense mass of colour in the hands of others. Using a dry brush, he dabbed and dragged the paper surface, conveying the light, soft texture of the creature's coat so ably.

Observing and drawing all his birds and beasts in the wild, Thorburn's colours are consistently true and therefore acceptable.

A. Thorburn
1919

Dormice

Watercolour 9¾ × 7¾in, signed and dated 1903
Original watercolour for *The Mammals of Great Britain and Ireland* by J. G. Millais, 1904–6, vol 2, plate 38

A fine example of a Thorburn book illustration, commissioned by Millais for his three-volume work *The Mammals of Great Britain and Ireland.* Thorburn painted a number of plates for this work, all of a similar high quality to the one shown here. Needless to say they were widely acclaimed.

Again the artist is seen excelling at composition, and his clever use of light and shade, rather than laborious detail, to give life and shape to his creatures. His decorative use of flowers and other accurate aspects of the countryside with which he enriched and enlivened his work is also seen. Note, for instance, the wild strawberry and the bee lurking beneath the leaves. How many would have thought of placing the merest drop of white (below the righthand creature's tail) to herald the yet to open bud of the wild strawberry?

Even as a very young man, Thorburn had perfected a technique for successfully depicting the fur, hair and feathers of the creatures he painted. Here, if we examine the dormouse closely, a series of expertly placed bands of wash are seen very quickly cross-hatched in darker tones which in turn immediately give birth to a living pulsating creature, enriched finally with convincing shape and form by the bold use of shadow.

The eyes of Thorburn's creatures are invariably superb and his dormice are no exception. The placing of the spot of white reflected light is consistently just right and, if facing the onlooker with two eyes shown, Thorburn will not forget to shadow one (as seen here) where the shape of the little creature's forehead and nose reduces the amount of light reaching the eye.

Such attention to detail set Thorburn well apart from his contemporaries, securing him there against the aspirations and efforts of those who have painted since.

Clearing after Rain

Watercolour 18 × 30¼in, signed and dated 1905
Red grouse sheltering in a peat hag

Huddled close together under a heathery bank, a small pack of red grouse awaits the rain to pass. As the shower slips away just as quickly as it came, shafts of sunlight break from the clouds, once more dappling the hillsides and coaxing the birds out of their sojourn.

Thorburn captures the scene so well. The grouse moor in autumn, 'red-brown wi' heather bells' as Burns admirably described it, gently formed out of hollow and crest, interspersed with indentation of track, upon which the birds shelter from the rain under the bank. Thorburn, well aware of the other importance to grouse of these old paths in providing them with their daily intake of grit so necessary for grinding the seeds and shoots in their crops, invariably incorporates them into his major paintings of red grouse. Indeed his titles for such pictures often allude to them – 'The Drove Road' and 'The Old Peat Track' being regularly used examples.

The quality of this work is typical of this period in his life, the birds being nicely and carefully attended to in his customary fashion. They stand firmly in a variety of postures, the one sheltering to the right emphasising the track along which one's eye is gently yet firmly led away into the swirling mists through which one can finally escape entirely from the picture.

This skilful construction of compositional painting effectively yet unobtrusively distances each passage of the picture, convincing the viewer of perhaps a full quarter of a mile between birds and ridge, all on the thickness of a sheet of paper.

Archibald Thorburn 1905

On the Stooks
Watercolour 21¼ × 29½in, signed and dated 1902
Blackgame feeding on the oat-sheaves

Thorburn loved blackgame and often depicted them feeding amid the oat stooks in the harvest fields of long ago. Flocks of a hundred birds or more were a common sight then. Sadly, today one would be well pleased to see a dozen or so together. In painting such pictures he faithfully captured for us a scene well nigh vanished from our landscape, swept aside by the so-called efficiency of more modern times, both in farming and in the afforestation of their habitat. At the same time such a scene as the one shown here serves as a natural history essay, complete in every detail. There are the high tops of the Scottish hills where the ptarmigan live and below them on the heather-clad slopes the red grouse. A little lower down sparse spinneys of birch trees grow and here, and upon the surrounding heathery moorland, the blackgame live.

At harvest time they have a bonanza and, flying over the old stone walls that divide the tilled ground from the wild moorland, regularly raid the cornfields, plundering man's meagre enough harvest in such high and austere places. At the first sign of danger they quickly rise amongst the sheaves, thereupon beating a hasty retreat to the safety of the heathery hollows beyond the old stone wall.

Thorburn's attention to detail abounds in this work. The feather lying uneasily awaits dispatch upon the breeze and the single stem of oats across the cock bird's tail, both add realism and a naturalistic touch. The painting of distance between the dark head of the cock bird set against the equally dark body of the hen bird is both very difficult yet equally successful.

One of Thorburn's greatest skills was knowing when to finish a picture, when to wash his brushes out and call it a day. Building a brick wall, everyone knows when it is complete. But with art no such obvious guide exists. Completion lies only in the eyes and hand of the artist. Here, highlighting the oats in the top righthand corner then down the righthand edge of the picture, finally scattering a handful across the bodies of the greyhens, so lovely are they that one could be forgiven for continuing the bombardment. However, such generosity would quickly topple the picture, so easily moving it from success and sheer delight to spoilage and contrivance.

Detail Whilst late September or even October would be considered late for England's harvest, such was the norm for the oat fields of Scotland, perhaps close to the Helmsdale on the east coast or in Glen Tromie close to Kingussie, two spots beloved by blackgame and Thorburn alike.

The cock bird, resplendent in his newly acquired blue-black feathers (having been in moult since July) together with his scarlet comb, feeds close to his much smaller and more sombrely clad mate, a greyhen.

How cleverly Thorburn blocks in two areas with bold layers of very dark paint yet prises the head of the blackcock neatly away from the almost equally dark body of the greyhen by the skilful placing of light.

This parting of the two masses of dark colour is further assisted by knowingly painting in one stalk of grain that unobtrusively threads its way between the birds.

Together the birds ravage the ripened grain, emphasised for us by the application of a much lighter colour. How competently the artist weaves degrees and areas of space between, around and under the birds by this simple yet most effective highlighting technique.

Archibald Thorburn
1902

Sparrow-hawk

Watercolour 14½ × 10¾in, signed and dated 1923
A male sparrow-hawk at the plucking perch whilst his mate hunts in the background

Undulating blue contours of distant heathland, topped with a scattering of windswept thorn trees so accurately sets the scene for this natural history lesson on sparrow-hawks, told with paint and paper. The distant bird flies fast and low across the countryside, hoping to surprise an unwary thrush, pipit or pigeon. If successful, the lesson tells us, the prize will be brought to the plucking perch, the branch of a fallen tree perhaps, where the unfortunate victim will quickly be defrocked, its feathers falling all around, some soon to drift aimlessly away upon the wind.

Thorburn's birds of prey are invariably keen-eyed, aggressive creatures. Devoid of humanisation and sentiment, they remain exactly what they are, dashing, astute, fearless, piercing-eyed predators, with an armoury of beak and claw pristinely kept.

Sparrow-hawks were often sketched from life in the wild by Thorburn. But, who knows, this one, like the eagle owl and the Iceland and Greenland falcons shown elsewhere in this book may well have originally been drawn in the aviaries at Lilford Hall some thirty years before this particular picture was composed and painted.

As a young man in his late twenties, Thorburn was a regular guest of Lord Lilford, one of the leading ornithologists of his day, and spent much time making innumerable sketches of the exotic birds his lordship kept at his extensive aviaries at Lilford Hall. The birds of prey particularly fascinated the young artist and most of his Greenland and Iceland falcon paintings of later years originated there.

This picture is yet another example of Thorburn's mastery of watercolour control with not the slightest hint of difficulty being encountered in any single passage of the painting.

Killed as He Reaches Cover

Watercolour 20 × 31in, signed and dated 1906
A peregrine falcon striking down a drake mallard as it makes for safety amongst the reeds

Wildly alarmed wildfowl, plunging at breakneck speed into the safety of the reeds, herald the closeness of a peregrine falcon scouring the wintry wilderness intent upon securing a meal before darkness once more closes in across the marsh.

With a resounding thud, the predator strikes a luckless mallard drake the merest moments before it reaches cover. The dead bird drops like a stone to the icy ground below, its feathers following silently as if in mourning for such an untimely death, there to await the talons and beak of the hungry bird as it swings sharply around and returns to claim its good fortune.

In the merest twinkling of an eye the episode was over. From silence through panic to silence, within seconds. Thorburn, able to mentally photograph the most intricate detail of such a fleeting moment, from position of head, wings, feet of both birds and feathers floating earthwards, records this winter scene with deadly accuracy and great distinction. From the swiftness of the peregrine's swoop as it continues rapidly by to the vertical plunge of the perished drake, the moment lives.

The glow of the setting sun is beautifully painted, its reflection not only being seen upon the snowbound marsh but, from there, also reflected upon the falcon's feathers.

Archibald Thorburn
1906

The Twelfth

Watercolour 30 × 51¾in, signed and dated 1906

Red grouse in full flight ahead of the guns on 12 August – the opening of the grouse-shooting season

At the first far-away echo a pack of red grouse come swinging by, disturbed at their feeding grounds by the sound of distant guns on the morning of 12 August.

This picture, surely one of Thorburn's finest achievements, so clearly demonstrates his skills in controlling watercolour over such a huge surface area. To put in such an enormous and compelling sky needs both courage and a deft hand, both of which Thorburn possessed in abundance.

Working at an easel, to begin painting in the top left-hand corner of such a large piece of paper, the colour needs to be applied quickly and confidently if it is to be successful and it can be seen how Thorburn achieved this, leaving sections of it to paint themselves (the paint running down across the already wetted paper) whilst he busied himself with the remainder. Moving to the right, the darkness steadily deepens, leaving the birds speeding ahead of the gunfire; or is it, one may well ask, thunder?

The shafts of light upon the distant moorland twinkle in the background and the birds themselves, solid, three-dimensional creatures that one can virtually cup with one's hands and remove from the paper, are enormously convincing, the swish of their wings can almost be heard as they speed on by over the heather in bloom.

Probably painted on the Perthshire hills whilst staying with his good friend J. Henry Dixon of Pitlochry (formerly of Inveran in Ross-shire), Thorburn knew such a scene intimately, being fully aware of the tilt of the grouse and the fickleness of the weather in such places, the short sharp showers frequently replenishing the peat pools as they passed by.

Although painted only a matter of years after his stays at Inveran on Loch Maree (where many of his grouse were drawn large in the landscape), here is a fine example of Thorburn constructing his flying grouse very much smaller in the overall composition to create a much more natural and pleasing work. Compare this picture to his flying grouse of a decade or so earlier, as shown on p18, and consider the different approach and technique as applied to the same subject, not only to the bird but the landscape as well.

Detail Most people by far, if given pencil and paper and asked to draw a bird, on the ground or in flight, would draw it side-on to the beholder. In this picture, however, is seen one of Thorburn's numerous skills as a painter expressed so eloquently in the angled pose of these two lovely red grouse as they wing by.

The sheer foreshortening technique of the leading bird is indeed a joy to the beholder, thrusting its head towards the viewer at the same time tucking its tail well back into the painting, gently leading us to view the birds following on behind.

One really feels the thickness of the muscle and the feathering of the righthand wing assembled by Thorburn through brilliant control of painting light and shade, forming its mould and shape. Another of the artist's regularly used tools of his trade can be seen clearly, namely his enviable ability at being able to portray distance in a picture by overlapping birds – or animals – as with the two grouse in question. The bird tucked in flight behind the tail of the leader immediately constructs depth into the flatness of the piece of paper and from there our eye automatically follows on, deeper into the painting, progressing to the more and more distant birds in the middle and far-off distance.

Finally, how well Thorburn keeps the birds above the ground by clever use of light and shade and very careful placing of the heather line below them.

Greenland Falcon

Watercolour 14¼ × 10½in, signed and dated 1913
Original watercolour for both the 1913 Christmas card and the signed limited edition print

Perched on a lofty lookout, a Greenland falcon surveys the vast wilderness that is its haunt. Far below, the tarn, upon which the wild duck live, reflects to perfection in its ice-cold crystal waters the towering crags above, over and through which these most noble of birds scour and hunt their prey.

Following its meal of mallard, the snow-white bird rests awhile whilst the unfortunate duck's feathers remain the only evidence of the recent kill, as they uneasily await dispatch upon the wind.

Thorburn was very fond indeed of these striking and gracious birds and nobody captured them better in paint than he. His very first drawings of them from life were made in the aviaries at Lilford Hall in the 1880s, when he was a regular guest of Lord Lilford of Northampton.

This particular watercolour, surely one of his finest (he chose it personally to be used as his Christmas card of 1913), may well be based on a Lilford sketch of twenty or twenty-five years earlier, or could, however, well be from another batch of drawings he produced of Greenland and Iceland falcons as a result of a number of visits to Regent's Park Zoo in the early part of the century.

The sharpness of eye, of beak and claw, are magnificently portrayed and Thorburn expertly weaves shape and solidity into the bird's form through clever use of shadow and light, not forgetting the wild, untamed nature of the creature in the process.

The hills in the background frame the bird, expertly leaving its head – the focal point of the picture – to protrude uncluttered. The hills also dip and fade, not meeting as a solid line, thus allowing a both pleasing and necessary escape from the painting.

Finally observe how cleverly Thorburn blocks in for us the progressive areas of distance into the work. The flying falcon convincingly splits the space between its closer mate and the hills beyond as it swoops downwards, inconspicuously adding an extra degree of distance into the picture.

A Hard Winter

Watercolour 21⅝ × 30⅜in, signed and dated January 1907
Wildfowl sitting out the frozen spell

Winter has laid its icy grip upon the landscape, not even the salt-laced river mouths escaping the squeeze.

Wildfowl gather at the still unfrozen pools to dip and preen, doze and feed, awaiting easier times. As dawn breaks across the icy marshland, casting its half-hearted rays of meagre warmth and hope, other birds fly in across the white wilderness in search of their life hole amid the ice.

Thorburn loved painting wildfowl almost as much as his beloved gamebirds, and, as with the gamebirds, particularly liked to depict them confronted and surrounded by the rigours and hardships of winter. He was a great exponent of winter skies and this is a particularly lovely example where all the colours of dawn are beautifully and knowingly reflected, not only upon the snows and pools below but from there reflected upon the birds themselves.

Again, observe his technique of distancing, where birds are placed strategically behind one another to lead one into the page. The three birds standing at the bottom-right are a fine example of this boxed and graded method of forming the picture and the bird swimming in the centre, where the casual nature of its bill remaining part hidden by the bank passes almost unnoticed, is yet again a brick in the building of distance.

Archibald Thorburn . Jany. 1907

Watched from Afar

Watercolour 22 × 30¾in, signed and dated 1910

Pheasants feeding at the edge of a larch wood

Watching intently, a resplendent cock pheasant keeps a wary eye upon two distant huntsmen. His head craned above the gorse thicket in which he and a hen bird hide, he quietly watches them approach.

Cleverly, having alerted the situation, Thorburn's narrative is about to return the scene to calm. For, looking closely, he bends the huntsmen to the left, skilfully indicating for us the path they are to take by the splash of sunlight that extends beneath the larch trees. Without that they could not head that way.

Compare the situation here, with its composition and its birds, with the picture 'Winter's Sunset' shown on p71. Notice the same diagonal constructional process, where the top line of the trees, running from left to right, meets the line of the path, in this case precisely pinpointing the position of the intruders on horseback.

Here, unlike many of Thorburn's countryside narrative pictures where one very often senses the presence of man yet does not see him, in fact man the disturber is seen and the reaction he brings forth from nature's creatures as the pheasants watch alertly, and the jay beats a hasty retreat into the safety of the autumn-dipped larches.

A delicious watercolour, marvellously controlled throughout by a man who knew and loved his landscape just as much as his birds and animals. Thorburn knew this spot well, a mere few minutes' walk from his Hascombe home and studio and often strolled along the path that meandered through the wood.

Highlighting the stems and heads of cocksfoot in the bottom corners of the work as he completed the picture, Thorburn, unlike most of us who, being so pleased with our efforts, would have painted just a few more to be followed by yet a few more, knew exactly when to wash his brushes out and finish.

There is a close similarity between this picture and 'Winter's Sunset' on p71 (also painted in 1910) in the construction as a whole. The birds in both are placed in the righthand half of the page looking towards the centre, with the cock pheasant in each standing on one leg. Each work carries a hen pheasant in the lefthand bottom corner as a balance to the composition.

One picture portrays an autumnal scene whilst the other the depths of winter, yet both are remarkably alike in their basic formation. The birds in both pictures are profiled small in the landscape, allowing the artist great scope and freedom in which to embellish the works with glorious yet carefully accurate renderings of their seasonal habitats.

Detail Comparing this detail with the one shown on p70 taken from 'Winter's Sunset', a considerable similarity is seen, both in posture as well as emphasis upon the birds, in the construction of both.

Again, in an unpretentious way, the cock bird's head is astutely placed against the buff-coloured background beyond, immediately leading one's eye to him, the principal bird, protecting the coy hens who lie low.

How well the invisible anatomy of the bird is built. The skeleton, upon which the feathers are draped, stands unfaltering, and tilted fractionally to the left, it perfectly counters the weight of the tail on the right, carried cleanly above the ground.

Such intricacies of perfection in natural history art are reserved for but a few. Only those who observed, and continue to observe, nature in all her varied moods and situations, would be aware of such minutiae that are of such major importance in getting the picture right.

Thorburn was the greatest exponent of expressing in his pictures a sound knowledge of such things. Many since his time are indebted to him for introducing them to the existence and importance of such components in the piecing together of a painting.

Archibald Thorburn
1910

Wrens at the Nest

Watercolour 10 × 7in, signed and dated 1923
A pair of wrens approach the entrance to their nest

Although Thorburn is best known for his paintings of gamebirds – pheasant, red grouse, partridge and so on, he was equally skilful at portraying the smaller birds of Britain. Here is seen that skill amply demonstrated in this delightful study of one of our smallest birds – the wren. His picture shows a pair of these dainty birds at their nest, a tiny bundle of bracken, leaves and grasses squeezed in at the base of a bush or small tree. The birds are exquisitely painted, quickly done, unencumbered with detail yet twinkling with alertness and vitality. The entrance hole to the nest is captured competently by cleverly placing the light coloured leaves overhanging the top of the cosy dark interior. As we see so often in Thorburn's work, his love of flowers is once more expressed, this time by decking out the foreground with blooms of winter aconite and leaves of ivy.

Such a work as this would take little more than a day to complete and Thorburn, unlike many artists, was well able to flick from wrens today to a bank of primroses tomorrow, followed by a Greenland falcon the day after, all handled with similar agility and with equal competence and success.

Again, if we dissect the painting, we observe the use of one base colour – this time brown – Thorburn skilfully prising out of it its entire range of tones, as he paints background and branch, birds and their nest.

Thorburn's creatures are always impeccably balanced, their centres of gravity correctly placed. Prior to Thorburn, who sketched every item in the field, most artists drew from skins, often faded and poorly mounted and very often with most unfortunate, unlifelike results.

Inconspicuously, yet of much importance in the overall composition, the patch of blue in the top lefthand corner allows us to escape from the confines of the wood.

Over the Hedge

Watercolour 30 × 51¾in, signed and dated 1907
A covey of partridge is disturbed and flies to the safety of the adjoining field

Disturbed whilst feeding, a covey of partridges quickly takes to the wing and, rising over a nearby hedge, drops down again almost immediately into the adjoining field where the birds will quickly be lost to view, their plumage blending remarkably with the landscape.

What a joy to see again such an untamed hedgerow from long ago, a refuge for all manner of plant and animal life and so necessary for the partridges in which to find sufficient cover to lay their eggs and hatch their young. Sadly, such scenes have dwindled dramatically since Thorburn's day and, with the disappearance of the traditional English hedgerow, the partridges have all but vanished too.

This huge watercolour, beautifully controlled throughout, from the hazy hint of distant hills to the vibrant, lush growth of the hedge and tree and flying birds, is a glorious recollection of times past. The birds themselves seem hardly necessary in such a lovely rendering of the English countryside just after the turn of the century. One senses the presence of man the disturber yet does not see him. The composition expertly leads the eye along the hedge from the bottom lefthand corner, turning left up through the birds who in turn lead us away towards the distant hills and the sky beyond.

Such enormous watercolours seemingly posed few problems for Thorburn and whilst, sadly, no complete list of his output exists, it would appear that he probably completed close on fifty works of this size (and even larger) during his lifetime. Whilst most were completed prior to 1905, examples do exist (as in this case) from later years.

Archibald Thorburn

Winter's Sunset

Watercolour 21 × 29in, signed and dated 1910
Pheasants feeding in a woodland ride at dusk in winter

The snow lies deep upon the woodland ride. A group of pheasants prepare for yet another bitter night amid the frozen branches. As the sun dips behind the trees, lengthening the shadows at the close of this winter's day, the birds seek their last morsel before winging up to their roost upon the bare boughs.

This marvellously atmospheric watercolour, capturing the crispness of the winter scene bathed in the glows of the setting sun, is one of Thorburn's finest achievements of one of his favourite situations and subjects. Knowing the wood intimately in all its varying moods, he excels at capturing the bleakness of the winter's day with snow upon the ground, the bushes bent under their load deposited by the recent fall. Thorburn captures the alertness of a cock pheasant in the stillness of the occasion, as the bird keeps a wary eye upon the path in case of marauding fox or other foe, whilst the two hen birds casually feed and preen before nightfall.

The composition is delightful, based upon diagonals once more, the skyline of trees tilting to the right and thus meeting the path angled upwards from both left and right.

Thorburn's pheasants are invariably gems of bird painting, the cock bird here being perfection indeed. Standing superbly, it exudes life and intensity with impeccably painted eye and tail gently held clear of the snow by the placing of shadow and footprint.

The frost-encrusted trees and bushes down along the ride emit an extra degree of chill, whilst the clear cold sun glints through the trees as it slips away over the edge of the land.

At about this time in his life (1910) Thorburn was producing some singularly lovely large spectacular watercolours of gamebirds in which he drew his birds relatively small within the overall composition. This technique enabled him to achieve a pleasing yet accurate exposition of a total country scene with the birds shown in their natural haunts rather than simply painting a map of a bird's plumage aided only by the slightest hint of background.

Note this approach succeeding equally well on pp67 and 79 in 'Watched from Afar' and 'The Morning Call' respectively.

Detail How crisply the cock pheasant's head stands clear of the woodland ride. With bold layers of paint, Thorburn quickly assembles its shape and twist, expert at introducing the sheen upon its neck as he goes. Almost at once, with a fine brush, he delicately laces and layers the feathers; not every one, preferring a hint here and there.

Limiting the use of his palette, how discreetly yet accurately he depicts both bird and bracken background, recording for us nature's hiding of the hen pheasant upon the woodland floor.

By such treatment – which Thorburn often employs – his pictures contain an overall harmonious effect, gentle and naturalistic, so unlike the blatantly artificial effect achieved by others using brash, sharp-edged, different colours, that bounce the eye about across the painting with much unease.

Compare this composition of cock and hen pheasant with that shown as a detail on p66. In each is clearly seen the protective assurance of the male bird and the distinctly more passive stance of his female companion, as though patiently awaiting instructions from her master.

Archibald Thorburn

Great Tits

Watercolour 10½ × 7¼in, signed and dated 1917

A pair of great tits amongst ivy

A charming study of these equally charming birds, known to us all whether we live our lives in the country or toil for our existence within the towns. Great tits, like their more numerous cousins the blue tit, appear to flourish whatever the habitat, both showing an affinity for man, unlike many of our birds and animals that show great fear.

Starting about 9.30 one morning during World War I, following his breakfast of porridge and his customary walk around his large and lovely garden, Thorburn, settling himself in his studio, would complete this work before sundown on the same day. Such was the speed and competence of the man that works of this size and quality were regularly produced from start to finish within the daylight hours of a single day.

People viewing and much enjoying his work often remark 'Isn't Thorburn's work detailed'. Well, actually it isn't. His skill is to imply detail without actually painting it. Examine closely the treatment afforded the principal bird. Extremely cleverly, a series of tonal washes are applied that, when dry, are highlighted and cross-hatched with a gradation of broad yet darker colour. Effectively and very quickly this not only forms the bird but gives it lightness and life as well. Compare this with the work of many who have followed and sought to better the master where excruciatingly heavy, laboured and cumbersome detail (many artists I'm sure tiling the poor birds with more feathers than they actually have!) simply topple the creature from reality into nothing more than a lifeless map of a bird's plumage, totally alien to the light, living, delicate creature of the wild.

Even here in such a small, almost mundane and very ordinary commission, Thorburn again feeds us the seed of narrative by tinting the sky with tones of dusk . . . or is it dawn?

Peacock and Peacock

Watercolour 34½ × 43¾in, signed and dated 1917

A peacock bird and peacock butterfly vie for decorative honours

Writing the obituary to Thorburn in the *Scottish Naturalist* of January 1936, Hugh S. Gladstone wrote '. . . but of all his pictures which I consider as the most daring was a gigantic one (4ft × 5ft, painted in 1915 for Mr Vincent C. Vickers) of a peacock in full display in front of a red rhododendron in full bloom; a gorgeous sunset and woodland as the background and, in the bottom lefthand corner, a peacock butterfly. My memory may be at fault as regards the details, but I remember the whole as a riot of colour; it was in no way displeasing but was both magnificent and accurate.'

Whilst opinions may well differ as to the validity of Gladstone's statement and which, if any, of Thorburn's achievements is in fact his finest, none will doubt the importance and extreme artistic merit of this amazing watercolour.

The work is huge in proportion as well as in attainment, and not a few artists would have encountered considerable difficulty in knowing just where to begin let alone how to control and complete such a feast of watercolour painting.

Several preliminary sketches were made in 1914 by Thorburn of the peacocks owned by the Vickers family, the final finished watercolour emerging and being delivered to them in 1917. It is possible that Thorburn worked on the picture from time to time over a period of perhaps six to twelve months or even longer, for Philip Rickman, who later owned the picture, related how Thorburn had told him of his restless nights as he dreamt over and over again of painstakingly painting the seemingly never-ending 'eyes' on the bird's plumage!

Rickman, himself an accomplished watercolour painter of birds, broadly shared Gladstone's view, marvelling at Thorburn's control throughout such a monumental challenge, particularly his painting green upon chinese white (without disturbing it) in order to achieve the scintillating iridescence of the feathers forming the base of the tail.

How well the bird stands, plucked from the background by bold and remarkable use of shadow below the bird and under its tail. And how well the composition balances, the red riot of rhododendrons on the right being countered by the escape to the bright blue world beyond on the left.

What of the peacock butterfly? Only Thorburn could have thought of such a delicate yet accurate touch. Not to be outdone by the enormity of the peacock's wings, the butterfly spreads its own beauty for all to see, bravely vieing for first prize.

The Bridle Path

Watercolour 22 × 29¾in, signed and dated 1910
Pheasants disturbed while feeding in Hascombe woods

Opening a gate at the bottom of his large and well-kept garden, Thorburn was able to step into some of the loveliest deciduous woodland in England. Acre upon acre of glorious trees and twisting tracks stretched before him, the paths edged with great sprawls of bracken which, in the autumn, seemed to set the woods ablaze.

Thorburn knew every inch of this place intimately and loved it dearly. The majority of his pheasant and woodcock sketches were made here, as well as countless others of smaller birds and mammals that dwelt within its confines.

In the middle of the wood, alongside the bridle path, stood an enormous tree, its shape and canopy quite distinctive and within its shadow grew a sapling. They both occur in several of Thorburn's major woodland pictures of pheasants, as a marker of this spot he loved so much and beneath and around which the woodland story revolved.

Thorburn walked this path regularly, almost daily at certain times of the year, filling his sketch books with hint of hawfinch, woodcock or common squirrel as well as pheasant. Sometimes, on his way home for lunch, he would call at the village shop and there be gently persuaded to share with others his briefest of sketches that told the woodland story so well.

'The Bridle Path' is one of his finest works from within the wood. One day, whilst watching and sketching a group of pheasants feeding undisturbed at the pathside, a screaming jay suddenly foretold of the approaching horse and huntsman, alerting the pheasants of the danger. Whilst without question a superb picture of pheasants in their own right, remarkably if we take the birds away, the picture remains scarcely spoilt, for the great tree and its canopy, surrounded by the bed of burnished bracken beneath, is in itself a joy to behold, reminding many of just such a place we recall with affection, perhaps from our childhood, or picnics long ago or courtship!

The picture is a fine example of how Thorburn subtly uses one base colour, exhausting every shade and hue within its compass, as he deftly decorates the landscape, correctly camouflaging the pheasants with the similar tones of the bracken they crouch within.

Detail The sheer alertness of the birds shown in this detail is a fine example of Thorburn's skill at not only being able to paint birds so beautifully but at capturing their attitude too, for alertness is expressed by attitude and stance.

Knowing his birds as well as he did, observing, learning and sketching them almost daily on his woodland walks or in his garden, Thorburn was so much more than a painter, being an expert naturalist as well.

Here there can be no doubt as to the presence of a disturber although, in this detail, the culprit is not seen. The angle of the birds' heads, the tilted tail of the bird on the right and their sheer intensity is captured to perfection. Asked to paint an alert pheasant, whilst many would make a commendable effort of coping with portraying the bird, most would find the alertness eludes them.

Archibald Thorburn 1910

The Finches

Watercolour 21 × 15½in, signed and dated 1915
Original watercolour for Thorburn's *British Birds*, 1915–16, vol 1, plate 16

One of Thorburn's many remarkable abilities was his skill in composing book illustrations, such as the one shown here, involving up to a dozen species or more upon a single page. Each was exquisitely drawn and finished within its own personal cameo invariably including a hint of its environment and yet together forming not only an overall acceptable and highly pleasing composition, where the hints of habitat blend unobtrusively together, but a stunningly beautiful and satisfactory picture eminently suitable for many a drawing room wall.

Thorburn didn't only love the birds and beasts of our countryside but its flowers as well and although the plate shown here is for a book on birds, it and almost all of the illustrations contain some botanical specimen discreetly yet deftly placed, adding an air of authenticity as well as charm to the work.

British Birds, published in 1915–16, was an instant success. Although Thorburn had illustrated a number of books prior to this, this was in fact the first he had both written and illustrated single-handed. It consisted of four volumes, together with a supplement published a little later, and in the first year following publication sold more than 1,000 copies. In all some 2,550 were sold, advertised by Longmans in their prospectus of the day at 6 guineas for the set! Many of the original plates were later sold by Thorburn upon return from his publishers, the proceeds of which he then generously donated to the Red Cross to assist their efforts during World War I.

Winter Tracks

Watercolour 7¼ × 10¾in, signed and dated 1913
Fox in winter

Tracks in the freshly fallen snow, deep and crisp and even, are carefully contemplated by a hungry fox. With all senses alert, the beast looks, listens and sniffs the taint upon the wind before stealthily emerging from the cover of the hedgerow out upon the sunlit snow. With hint of distant hedge and snow-bound meadow, Thorburn captures the winter's day long ago with great economy of effort yet with equally great effect.

Again the narrative is there. Something has just happened – a hare or rabbit has passed this way – and something else is about to happen. The story must be unravelled together.

Thorburn also expertly captures the timidity of the fox, commonly incorrectly portrayed by others as wild and aggressive. His sense of texture clearly differentiates between the hair of the animal, the prickles of the gorse and the evenness of the snow. The angle of the light and the lie of the land are all there for one to see, so convincing that one could be excused for forgetting that one is looking at a painting at all, considering it to be the scene itself.

Thorburn was a remarkable painter of time and weather, often adding to his pictures these extra dimensions of time of day and temperature, which so enrich his work.

This watercolour would constitute a typical day's work for the artist. Commissioned to paint a fox in the snow, Thorburn, taking a piece of his already meticulously cut paper, would refer to sketches of foxes made in Hascombe woods and elsewhere and select one for the job in hand. Copying it from sketch book to paper, he would quickly add an appropriate hint of background of hedge. Following the minimum use of pencil work, the paint would begin to flow on in well under an hour and, long before the end of the day, the work would be completed.

Archibald Thorburn
1913

The Morning Call

Watercolour 21 × 29in, signed and dated 1911
Red grouse awakening on the Scottish moors

As the sun slowly emerges above the distant hills, casting its welcome glow upon the Scottish hillsides, a pack of red grouse awakens, the old cock bird acknowledging both the break of day and a neighbouring pack of birds, incoming from adjoining heathery slopes.

The picture is a very lovely yet typical rendering of a scene that Thorburn knew intimately and recorded equally well on countless occasions with paint upon paper. Such a work and of this size and quality would normally take him less than a week to complete and perhaps fifty such superlative efforts of red grouse on the moors were painted, many between 1905 and 1915.

On his annual visits to Scotland, Thorburn would return to certain locations time and time again, filling his sketch books with hints of the birds and the backgrounds that would later re-emerge, redrawn and expertly painted on larger pieces of paper, destined to decorate the drawing rooms of a fortunate few.

Red grouse were especially drawn during his painting stays at Inveran on the shores of Loch Maree in Ross-shire, as well as at Pitlochry in Perthshire and again at Gaick. Certain landmarks appear quite regularly in the construction of the backgrounds of these fine watercolours (as for example the pointed hill at Gaick), thus identifying the location at which the particular picture was originally drawn.

In this picture again observe Thorburn's skill at laying on beautifully controlled washes of sky, hills and loch, of his ability to distance the narrative in his work and his articulate use of space. Noting again the unobtrusive placing of the main bird's head against a light band of colour within the sky, we realise the subtlety of this technique as we visualise the loss of impact had the head been placed against the darker band of cloud.

Thorburn was a great atmospheric painter and revelled in depicting the creatures of the countryside at dusk or dawn. Many of his important pictures carry evocative titles relating to the time of day, as here for example with 'The Morning Call'. Turning to p53, in 'Morning', Thorburn once more reveals red grouse framed against the first light of day and 'A Frosty Dawn' on p85, and 'Sunrise over Gaick' on p39 are further fine examples of his fascination for the breaking day and his aptitude at capturing and portraying it resplendent with watercolour.

Detail Thorburn captures so well the aggressiveness of the old cock red grouse as his morning call shatters the stillness of the autumnal dawn.

The bird's attention has been claimed by the incoming pack of grouse (not shown in the detail), in front of which he now assumes responsibility for his own pack, quietly sitting and pecking around him, by drawing himself up to full stretch upon a pinnacle of rock and vehemently voicing his presence.

Once more see Thorburn's beautifully fluent and rapid technique of feathering his birds. Avoiding cumbersome detail, notice how the basic solid bands and blocks of colour are given shape and 'detail' merely by a change of tone as the painting progresses, leaving only some quick-fingered and delicate flecking of feathers to be done with darker paint.

How well the bird stands. Note how successfully the two little panels of light beneath the bird and behind its legs lift it clear of both background and rock.

The Forester's Friend

Watercolour 5½ × 4in, signed and dated 1925
A great spotted woodpecker. The original for the RSPB Christmas card of 1925

Thorburn painted this charming little watercolour for the RSPB's Christmas card of 1925. Even though such a small work would rarely take him more than half a day to complete, it nevertheless lacks none of his characteristic flair and touch. From the beautifully controlled washes of the background to the quick impression of the pine needles clustered around the rotten tree stump, each section carries his stamp of distinction, whilst the bird itself is a little gem, painted with the minimum of strokes yet with the maximum of effect, vibrantly alive and solid, so obviously gripping the trunk by toe and tail.

In all Thorburn painted some nineteen Christmas cards for the RSPB, beginning with one of roseate terns in 1899 (accompanied by a poem by Alfred Austin, the Poet Laureate of the day), and ending with one of a goldcrest, completed with great difficulty yet characteristic determination, whilst he lay painfully and terminally ill in bed at his home in 1935.

The originals for the Christmas cards he then donated to the society, some if not all being duly sold to help raise funds to purchase some of the very first bird reserves. For his generous contribution towards bird preservation, Thorburn was elected a vice-president of the society in 1927.

Eiders and Scoters

Watercolour 13½ × 18½in, signed and dated 1921
Original watercolour for Thorburn's *Gamebirds and Wildfowl of Great Britain and Ireland*, 1923, plate 23

One almost feels the swell and hears the slap of the sea as the raft of eiders and scoters rides the waves. This work, painted for Thorburn's book *Gamebirds and Wildfowl of Great Britain and Ireland* of 1923 truly reflects his intention in this particular work to portray the birds in their natural environments.

The birds are restless, unnerved by the rising wind and sea echoed by the darkening sky and swirling gulls and almost encouraged to leave now by the sudden departure of the scoters, flying away out of the picture.

The painting of water in watercolour, particularly the sea, constantly poses problems for an artist for the final version has very largely to be achieved by the laying on of the initial washes. With wetted paper, Thorburn flows in the sky loose and free, adding pigment as he progresses to thus emphasise the storm approaching from the right. Quickly, before it dries, with a rag he removes small passages for effect, including a flurry of finger dabs in the top righthand corner.

Then on with the sea. With bobbing horizon bounced by the wind, he fluently and very quickly lays on an array of tones, skilfully using the angles of the birds to construct the swell, finally highlighting with white the crests of the waves. Imagine how he approached capturing the splattering spray midway down the righthand side of the picture and how easily it could have been a disaster.

The various groups of birds gradually build distance into the work for the viewer, the two birds in the foreground with their backs to us adding considerably to this effect as they swim into the middle distance of the painting, creating both depth and movement.

From the gulls wheeling into the scene from the right to the ducks departing from it on the left, the whole picture abounds in movement. Scanning the vast surging sea to the distant heaving horizon, no stillness can be seen.

Archibald Thorburn 1921.

Danger Aloft

Watercolour 21 × 30in, signed and dated 1927
Ptarmigan in autumn plumage at Gaick in Inverness-shire

Emerging from the mists boiling up out of the corrie at the head of the glen, a golden eagle drifts lazily along the ridge at Gaick, startling the herd of red deer quietly browsing at the rim of the great cauldron and alerting the pack of ptarmigan feeding amongst the rocks. The birds crouch and 'freeze', their plumage blending well with the boulders and vegetation of such high places, and await the danger aloft to pass.

A truly superlative example of Thorburn's skills as a watercolour painter and naturalist. The background colours are flowed on wet and with great speed, fresh tones being added every few seconds as he works quickly across the paper. The mists are a remarkable achievement, attained by alternately applying paint and then removing sections of it with a cloth until the desired effect is achieved. The merest hint of pink in the sky draws one's eye to the gliding bird, at the same time linking in the red eye patches of the old cock ptarmigan and the blueberry within the overall composition. The ptarmigan, drawn in the most difficult yet realistic of positions, are masterpieces of bird art, extremely successful in their foreshortening and convincing shape, so alive yet unburdened with cumbersome detail.

The scene, painted at Gaick, is timeless and as long as deer, eagles and ptarmigan are allowed to remain in such eternal places, it will bear meaning and truth for generations to come.

The composition cleverly leads our eye from the righthand bottom corner of the work through the pack of birds, along the rim of the cauldron, picking up the deer on the way (not forgetting the straggler on his way down from the summit) and so along the ridge to the eagle, emerging from the mists.

Thorburn loved both ptarmigan and the wilderness in which they live. Their ever-changing plumage coinciding with the colours of the seasons never ceased to fascinate and inspire him. Here we see the sombre colours of autumn in such high places. Compare the same situation but enduring the ice-capped conditions of winter in his painting on p39. Enormous distance is built into the work, Thorburn cleverly using curving hillsides to guide us. Notice how, with the merest of strokes, he aptly captures the fear of the hinds as they contemplate the marauder in the sky.

Detail The dramatic quality of much of Thorburn's largescale work considerably sharpened the narrative content of his pictures. Here the swirling mists blotting out the rim of the corrie, whilst remaining true to the situation, at the same time most effectively involve another spectacle into the overall composition adding to the intensity of the moment.

How rapidly and fluently Thorburn lays on the paint, both on birds and background. With relatively broad brush strokes, he races away across the background, throwing in a splash of darker hue here and a lighter one there. Almost before dry, he adds a fleck or two with a finer brush, hinting at herbage or cleft amongst the stones, leaving the whole thing invigorating and free, on the move, developing by the moment completely untied down by time.

Thorburn the naturalist tells us that ptarmigan, unlike most birds, squat at the approach of danger, relying upon their excellent camouflage – both here in autumn and on p49 in winter ('The Shadow of Death') to protect them from predators.

Observe how quickly and neatly Thorburn shapes the birds' heads, most shown in the most difficult of positions, by picking out in white and blocking in with shadow.

A. Thorburn
1927

Blue, Marsh and Long-tailed Tits

Watercolour 11 × 7¼in, signed and dated 1924
Original watercolour for Thorburn's *British Birds*, 1925–6, vol 1, plate 24

Although one of the aims expressed by Thorburn for his four-volume *British Birds* of 1925–6 was to depict as many species as possible in their natural environments, allotting wherever he could a page to each, this plate, like several others, does show three species upon one page, albeit in their natural environments and in very convincing and characteristic poses. In his earlier work on *British Birds*, published in 1915–16, many species were shown on each page, each accompanied by the merest environmental hint as its own particular background.

Painted on pale brown paper, the background of this work is exquisitely put in free and flowing, a masterly example of light and shade and of highlighting, yet not at all obtrusive, retaining its prime purpose of being complementary to, and not master of, the subject of the picture, namely the birds themselves. These are round and solid, each in turn endowed with its own characteristic and pose, as any bird watcher would confirm. The ebullient blue tit, the shy, retiring marsh tit and the secretive long-tailed tit, Thorburn captures the nature of each so well.

Again here is a fine example of a composition based on a pronounced use of diagonals, each leading us to the next passage of the painting. As in so much of his work, Thorburn's subtle and pleasing technique of involving the use of one or two base colours with which to tint both bird and background is so thoroughly expressed. These he then skilfully unwraps, extricating every shade and tone possible from within their inventory. Notice the browns and buffs, greys and mauves that flow over from fronded background upon feathered birds.

A Frosty Dawn

Watercolour 22¼ × 30in, signed and dated 1927
A covey of partridge awakening upon the frost-gripped stubble

Lapwings rise above the frost-laden stubble and fly towards the brightening dawn. Below an old cock partridge rasps out his early morning welcome to just another day, whilst his covey, awakening in such inhospitable conditions, preens and begins to feed upon the frost-gripped fare.

Thorburn captures this moment at first light beautifully, balancing the delicacy of the dawn upon the wintry landscape with the harsh reality of the situation, the birds fluffed out against the bitter cold as they search for meagre morsels.

In a series of lovely pastel shades, the receding night sky gives way to the approaching dawn, the birds boldly drawn and firmly placed upon the stubble. Four out of the five principal birds are drawn head or tail on to the viewer, all of which, whilst most difficult to achieve, are most convincing, the bird on the far right being particularly so. Whichever section of the painting one contemplates, one's eye is immediately drawn to the crowing cock bird whose head is strategically placed against the brightening sky. The foreground is both superbly and unusually handled, much of it being boldly dragged with broad brushfuls of colour, deftly brought into perspective by the highlighting of stems of stubble, together with their accompanying shadows, and the clover leaves, one half pecked. Notice how, with bold streaks of paint, Thorburn quickly and most confidently completes the plumage of the birds, flecking their flanks with buff. As always the birds' eyes are most carefully attended to and although on each of the birds in the foreground only one eye is seen, one is nevertheless fully aware of the other.

Although painted more than thirty years after 'The Covey at Daybreak' of 1892, (see p45), Thorburn still discreetly leads our eye to the old cock bird in charge of the covey by astutely placing the head against a light band of colour in the sky. Once again this seemingly casual yet carefully calculated technique is seen on p89 in 'The Upland Stubbles' of 1920.

A. Thorburn
1927

Through the Snowy Coverts
Watercolour 14¾ × 22in, signed and dated 1926
Blackgame returning to their winter roost at dusk

Winging their way homewards beneath a wintry sky, blackgame return from their feeding grounds on nearby moorland slopes. Tilting first this way and then that, skilfully they thread their way through the white-limbed trees as they make for their snug retreat amongst the silver birches.

The setting sun lights their way home, casting its rosy glow upon the woodland pool which, in turn, ricochets it back again upon the underparts of the passing greyhen, tinting her too with the setting sun.

One senses the swish of their wings as the birds hurry by, leaving the place to assume an eerie silence as the sun fades and the dusk settles amongst the snow-clad trees.

Thorburn knew these birds like no other person, revelling in capturing in watercolour the electric-blue sheen and lyre-shaped tail of the handsome male birds and the sombre buffs and browns of the so-called 'greyhen'. He also regularly trod their habitat. Clad in stout, warm clothes, mittens preventing his fingers from freezing, he sketched them on numerous occasions 'packing' on the snows of winter before flying home to roost.

Thorburn's snow scenes are invariably compelling and atmospheric gems of watercolour painting, constructed on a sound knowledge based on long and careful observation of reflected lights upon the snow, of grey and blue shadows and of his awareness of snow rarely, if ever, being snow white.

Flying birds are difficult to paint successfully and Thorburn, like all others, never found them easy. Here, however, we see skills possessed by but a few as the birds convincingly swing through the trees at considerable speed.

Detail Birds in flight have always posed a problem for artists; more often than not, in the hands of most painters, they remain unmoving as if suspended on wires. Indeed some artists have been known to admit constructing such a scene in their studios resorting to this method, but, alas, all to no avail.

However, in the days before the advent of fast, accurate natural history photography there was little an artist could do other than concoct and fabricate the flying bird. Unless that is, of course, one was fortunate enough to possess the visual memory of Thorburn and indeed of George Lodge.

Flying by, often at great speed, it was only Thorburn's gift in this direction, combined with his intimate field knowledge of the birds he was portraying, that enabled him to pluck them from that fleeting moment, calling up from his memory the positions of wings and tail, the placing of head and feet and the angle of its anatomy.

No hidden wires here, as the greyhen hurries through the wood positively thrusting her way forward, piercing the crisp air like an arrow.

A. Thorburn
1926

The Common Squirrel

Watercolour $9\frac{3}{4} \times 7\frac{3}{4}$in, signed and dated 1903
Original watercolour for *The Mammals of Great Britain and Ireland* by J. G. Millais, 1904–6, vol 2, plate 37

Around the turn of the century, when this picture was painted, the red squirrel abounded in the woodlands of Britain. At that time the grey squirrel had yet to be introduced to our shores and the red, or common squirrel as it was known then, for there was no other, had the woods to itself. With the introduction of its American cousin however, followed by its rapid spread and colonisation of our countryside, the common squirrel of the past has become very much the uncommon of the present, harassed and overpowered by its grey counterpart and forced, sadly, into decline. Woods that abounded with them in Thorburn's day have been without them for many years now.

The splendid watercolour shown here, painted on commission to J. G. Millais as an illustration for his book *The Mammals of Great Britain and Ireland*, depicts a pair of these delightful creatures alertly feeding amongst the branches. One stands upright stripping a nut with the aid of nimble feet and sharp teeth whilst balancing deftly with gripping toes and quivering tail. Besides ably aiding its balance as it bounds amongst the branches, the bushy tail provides the squirrel with a warm wrap in winter as it slumbers away the briefest and coldest days, curled snugly in its drey amid the bare swaying treetops.

The Upland Stubbles

Watercolour 20×30in, signed and dated 1920
A covey of partridge enjoys the warmth of the autumn sunshine

On the brow of a hillside stubble field a partridge covey quietly and lazily feeds on the ample spilled grain left by the recent harvesters. Enjoying the warmth of the soft autumn day, from their high vantage point the birds keep a wary eye on the fields tumbling away below them, rolling away to the distant blue-lined hills that merge with the clear blue sky of such a perfect day.

Whilst some feed and others doze, one old cock bird keeps a sharp eye open on all he surveys, lest danger lurks, recognising the approaching birds as a neighbouring covey of his own kith and kin.

A lovely composition executed with great skill as a painter, clearly expressing the artist's compassion for his subject. At this period in his life, Thorburn was fluent and free, floating colour across the page with great ease and conviction. He loved partridge, often showing them upon the stubbles of autumn or enduring the bleak times of winter.

How skilfully he uses the one palette of basic colour to correctly tint the landscape that in turn effectively camouflages the birds living upon it. As a direct yet beautiful contrast, he explores the shades of blue with which to not only put in the sky but the gradations of hills and far-off fields as well.

The strong use of shadow neatly separates the birds, at the same time lifting them clear of the ground. The hewn-down thistle, lying prostrate upon the field, is further evidence of the recent passing of the harvest flail as well as recalling days long before the advent of the spray can.

Archibald Thorburn
1920

Woodcock & Chicks
Watercolour $7\frac{1}{2} \times 11$in, signed and dated 1932
Woodcock family concealed upon the woodland floor

Resting quietly upon the flower-decked woodland floor, a woodcock broods her young. Amid last year's dying leaves, this year's new arrivals take their first few steps, though not daring to stray too far from the comfort and safety of their parent's wings.

The adult bird, expertly camouflaged by instinct and nature, broods her young, crouched close against the lichen-covered fallen tree. Alert yet secretive, she keeps a wary vigil for that first far-away echo that could spell danger.

Thorburn was a master at utilising the space of a painting to the maximum, leading one's eye, as he does here, across the page through a series of diagonals.

Although he painted many pictures of woodcock, one of his favourite birds, this must surely rank as one of Thorburn's finest of the bird. Painted in just over a day at the age of seventy-two and seriously ill with cancer, it was purchased for £10 by Philip Rickman, the bird artist, when visiting his great friend and teacher one day in 1932.

The boldness of colour laid on as the background is both striking and beautiful, setting off the foreground to great effect. Thorburn had a marvellous understanding of colour harmony and a great sense of texture, being able to capture the feel of a leaf, feather, or fur with equal ease and success. He also excelled at using light to centre and highlight the subject of the painting and used strong shadow to lift one section away from others, as here the bird's beak is clearly parted from its breast below. Although Thorburn's studio was festooned with all manner of lovely pictures that day in 1932, Philip Rickman chose this small one of woodcock as the finest of them all.

Detail With the predominance and, so it seems, preference for heavily and laboriously detailed representations of the birds and animals of our countryside currently in vogue, the backgrounds of such pictures invariably suffer from the same over-photographic approach. Such treatment of bird, beast and background effectively robs the work of any germ of spontaneity, leaving the picture flat, morose and, more often than not, quite unreal.

Thorburn's work, however, shows none of this laboured, pernickety approach and survives unscathed from the past because of this freedom, with its vitality and freshness, totally devoid of tiled birds and paved backgrounds. He relies on hint, rather than hard fact, with which to form the living scene and in this small detail is seen an exquisite example of this technique as the little fronds of bracken hang delicately against the richness of the background yet are not suspended by, nor attached to, anything. Blot them out however and the picture loses so much of its freedom and spontaneity. On the other hand, link them tediously together in chain-like fashion to other fronds and even to more and more, and the clinical and cluttered technique would be seen, so much in fashion right now, losing the picture's freshness and vitality in the process.

Time naturally determines the long-term appeal of art, but Thorburn, I feel sure, having survived and flourished with great distinction over the past hundred years has little to fear from the next hundred. His beautifully artistic yet totally accurate impressionistic gems of our countryside will continue to please and satisfy those who contemplate his work and inspire and encourage those who seek to emulate it.

A. Thorburn 1932

Ptarmigan at Sunrise

Watercolour 14¼ × 21in, signed and dated 1910
Ptarmigan in the snow at Gaick in Inverness-shire

Most of Thorburn's drawings of ptarmigan originated on the estate of Gaick in Inverness-shire. He first stayed there in 1889 as a young man of twenty-nine and subsequently returned as a visitor each autumn for many years. It was here that he saw his first live red deer as well as his first ptarmigan, and he loved the place immensely. The wild, untamed vastness of it inspired him to produce some scintillating atmospheric renderings of the place clearly seen in this very fine watercolour.

Consider for a moment the challenge of painting white birds in snow upon white paper, and in watercolour! Thorburn, however, not only accepted the challenge but revelled in its demands and his achievements of such subjects are invariably remarkable. This picture is typical of his attainment, showing a pack of these lovely snow-white birds at sunrise amid the snowy wastes of such high places.

Gaick has a pointed hilltop and whenever a picture of ptarmigan, red deer or golden eagle originated there, a pointed ridge appears in the composition. Artistic licence decrees that its outline varies from picture to picture but, nevertheless, it is as sure and dependable at pinpointing the place as seeing the word 'Gaick' carefully inscribed alongside his signature and date.

The whole work is handled most delicately, with beautiful control of the sky and snow, the bold blue shadows quickly positioning the birds whilst at the same time clearly showing the angle of the land amongst which they shelter and feed.

Notice Thorburn's truth in showing each bird in a different pose and angle, some most difficult to achieve, and the flying birds, swiftly gliding in across the snowy wastes, enrich the picture with great movement.

Detail To succeed in creating the realism of a pack of white ptarmigan high up on the snows of winter using white paint upon white paper, calls for a very rare talent indeed. Whilst in this detail, Thorburn places the birds upon a slab of wind-blown, snow-free ground to create a pleasing yet accurate contrast in tonal composition, nevertheless much of the white bird is framed against a backcloth of white snow, presenting very considerable problems of distinction.

Upon careful examination, however, there is another reason for incorporating such a slab of snow-free rock, as the reflected lights of snowy places bounce some of the rocky hues back upon the birds themselves, much assisting Thorburn in plucking them clear of the white wasteland beyond.

Thorburn loved depicting these beautiful birds in their bleak surroundings, revelling in the challenge posed by nature of unwrapping and disclosing for all to see that which she seeks to keep from us by camouflaging her creatures so well.

Archibald Thorburn 1910

Voices of the Forest

Watercolour 21¼ × 29½in, signed and dated 1912

Red deer stag roaring across the glens of Gaick

Thorburn saw and sketched his first wild red deer at Gaick in Inverness-shire in 1889. At the time he was staying there as a house-guest on the estate. During the same visit he also encountered his first ptarmigan following an early Sunday morning climb. The vast isolation of Gaick enthralled him and he was to return annually for many years to come, making the epic journey by train from London to Kingussie and from there to the lodge, a journey of some twelve miles or so through the glens, by pony and trap.

'Voices of the Forest', painted in 1912, although one of many red deer pictures he was to paint at Gaick (the pointed mountain top indicates this particular locality), is surely one of his finest. He captures so well the height of the ridge on which the stag stands and roars, the landscape dropping steeply into the chasm below, with its tumbling torrent twisting its way out of the hills and into the sunlit glen beyond.

The red deer itself stands superbly, drawn as it is in a most difficult foreshortened position. Cleverly placed within the lefthand half of the picture, Thorburn leaves the right-hand side free to depict the wildness of the landscape and the skein of geese high in the sky, honking their way westwards towards the setting sun and their roost upon the shore. His skies invariably capture the mood of such high places with marvellous cloud and mist effects boiling up out of corries. Laying on brushfuls of colour, he would proceed to rub off sections with a rag until the desired effect was achieved. The breath of this particular roaring stag, far from being paint laid on was also achieved by colour being taken off.

As so often in a Thorburn painting one senses other things and the passage of time, setting his pictures apart from those of other wildlife painters. Other deer lurking in the background, just out of sight maybe, and, as the geese fly westwards towards the setting sun, the inevitability of the dusk to come. Such additional dimensions to his work are a reason to return regularly to contemplate anew his scenes lest some things have been missed.

If asked to draw a stag on a hilltop, how many out of the first hundred people met and asked would have drawn it thus? I would guess none, expecting all to opt for the easy solution and draw the beast side on. Drawing it as Thorburn does (taken from an original sketch, as indeed was all his work) tail towards the viewer, head looking into the picture and thereby cleverly guiding us to the Gaick hilltop and the flying geese beyond, requires much skill at foreshortening, skilfully distancing the head from the tail, the whole beast standing superbly, knowingly propped by the artist by the unseen yet accurate compilation of the animal's centre of gravity.

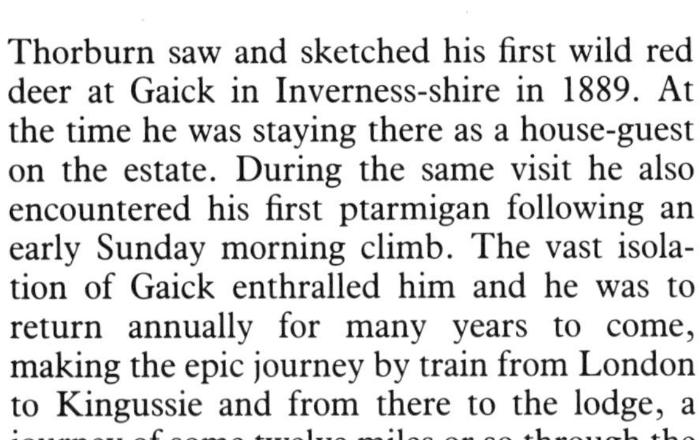

Detail Standing high on the ridge, the stag roars its presence down the length of the glen, its tones mingling with the cascading river and the honking of the geese. Together their voices form the music of the deer forest.

Thorburn's draughtsmanship is superb, the beast angled first to the left, from tail along its back, and then to the right, along the neck to the focal point, its head and particularly the eye.

The drawing is then clothed with paint through which the animal's shape and form emerge, aided by light and shade. The harmony of colour tones are once again apparent as Thorburn cleverly shades background and beast from a limited palette.

Thorburn the observer knows just the angle of the head and neck and the laid-back ears as the stag emits his deep bellow across his domain.

Woodcock Glade *(overleaf)*

Watercolour 11 × 14¾in, signed and dated 1923

Woodcock resting in a wood in autumn. Original watercolour for limited edition print published in 1923

Thorburn loved woodcock and painted a multitude of pictures of them. Varying considerably in shape, size and situation, some birds are shown in the snows of winter whilst others enjoy more congenial times. All are singularly lovely representations of one of his favourite birds, for nobody ever painted woodcock better.

Here the warmth of the autumn sun enhances the glowing colours of the birch wood in the fall of the year. The riot of background colours are flowed on fast and wet, mingling harmoniously, again Thorburn well nigh exhausting every hue and tint from a base colour of brown.

Compared to his work of earlier years where every frond of bracken would be painstakingly painted (see p35), now at the height of his powers he simply transforms his mix of background washes into bracken by the merest stroke of shadow and gives birth to birch trees by simply limbing them white. The birds themselves, though well finished, are not burdened with cumbersome detail, remaining alive and vibrant, the main bird standing well clear of the background.

More than likely the original sketch for this work – published by Embleton and signed by Thorburn as a limited edition print in 1923 – would have been made in Hascombe woods, a mere ten minutes' walk or so from his studio.